AF412170

DAO of Managing Higher Education in Asia

DAO of Managing Higher Education in Asia

Yu Sing Ong

Southern University College, Malaysia

NEW JERSEY · LONDON · SINGAPORE · BEIJING · SHANGHAI · HONG KONG · TAIPEI · CHENNAI · TOKYO

Published by

World Scientific Publishing Co. Pte. Ltd.

5 Toh Tuck Link, Singapore 596224

USA office: 27 Warren Street, Suite 401-402, Hackensack, NJ 07601

UK office: 57 Shelton Street, Covent Garden, London WC2H 9HE

Library of Congress Cataloging-in-Publication Data
Names: Yu, Sing Ong, author.
Title: Dao of managing higher education in Asia / Yu Sing Ong,
    Southern University College, Malaysia.
Description: New Jersey : World Scientific, [2016]
Identifiers: LCCN 2016053358 | ISBN 9789813203006 (hardcover) |
    ISBN 9813203005 (softcover)
Subjects: LCSH: Universities and colleges--Asia--Administration. |
    Education, Higher--Asia. | Educational change--Asia.
Classification: LCC LB2341.8.A76 O64 2016 | DDC 378.1/01095--dc23
LC record available at https://lccn.loc.gov/2016053358

British Library Cataloguing-in-Publication Data
A catalogue record for this book is available from the British Library.

Desk Editor: Edward C. Yong

Typeset by Stallion Press
Email: enquiries@stallionpress.com

Printed in Singapore

To my lovely wife, Jesslyn,
and my two loving daughters, Yvonne and Michelle

Contents

Preface

This book is written as a compendium, with each chapter logically connected to the others, with the connecting thread of "efficacy" in education management. As the title suggests, it is intended as a reference guide for administrators and researchers. It looks at issues from a strategic management viewpoint and analyses problems from a business process reenginering perspective. While the various chapters may include data analysis on specific research topics, this book does not aim to be a quantitative analysis book. It is the author's opinion that it would be counter-productive to create a tome on research methodologies as the focus on this book is on managing higher education in Asia.

The book begins with a review of the differences in perspectives between Western and Eastern researchers in their approach to conducting research. The subsequent chapters serve as a practical guide to Higher Education Institutions (HEIs) administrators and leaders who are actively involved in setting the direction of their institutions. It covers relevant theories and specific research topics to provide a comprehensive view on private HEIs in Singapore and Malaysia. Students will also be able to gain a good insight into the research methodologies applicable to analyse HEIs.

The eight chapters of this book cover:

(1) Reexamining Education Research Methodologies.
(2) Readdressing Key Challenges Facing Higher Education Institutions.
(3) Reinforcing Regulation of Private Institutions.
(4) Reculturing Private Universities.
(5) Reevaluating Teaching Effectiveness.
(6) Remaking the University as an Institution of Choice.
(7) Reframing Absentee Rate.
(8) Reinventing Principal Leadership.

Acknowledgements

I would like to thank Professor Wong Yoon Wah for his encouragement and support to me in writing this book. He has been a great motivator and mentor to me. I would also like to extend my appreciation to Dr Thock Kiah Wah who has provided me with an exciting insight into managing a largely Chinese-oriented university. I also wish to express my deepest thanks to Professor Phua Kok Khoo, Chua Hong Koon and their colleagues at World Scientific Publishing for their guidance in launching this book.

About the Author

Associate Professor Yu has over 29 years of senior management experience in banking, research, consulting and education. He started his career in Wall Street, New York, in the 1980s. Following his return to Singapore, he was instrumental in establishing and managing the Investment Management unit of a pension fund. He was appointed the Research Director of a major local bank and the Regional Vice-President of Investment Banking of an international bank.

As an entrepreneur, Associate Prof. Yu established three companies, specialising in consultancy, project management and education services. He has provided advisory services to over five hundred private and public companies in Singapore, Philippines, Thailand, Malaysia, Vietnam and Indonesia.

His desire to share his knowledge and experience led him to join the education sector in 2004. He has held senior positions at three universities in Vietnam and Malaysia and a Private Education Institution in Singapore. Associate Prof. Yu graduated with a Doctorate in Business and a Doctorate in Arts Management. He is also a Certified Financial Planner in Malaysia.

企者不立; 跨者不行; 自見者不明; 自是者不彰; 自伐者無功;
自矜者不長。其在道也, 曰: 餘食贅行。物或惡之,
故有道者不處

He who stands on his tiptoes does not stand firm; he who stretches his legs does not walk (easily). (So), he who displays himself does not shine; he who asserts his own views is not distinguished; he who vaunts himself does not find his merit acknowledged; he who is self-conceited has no superiority allowed to him. Such conditions, viewed from the standpoint of the Dao, are like remnants of food, or a tumour on the body, which all dislike. Hence those who pursue (the course) of the Dao do not adopt and allow them.

Dao De Jing

Chapter 1

Reexamining Education Research Methodologies

This chapter examines the dominance of Western research methodologies and suggests that they may not fully address research studies on Eastern cultures. It begins with a broad overview of the influences of Western philosophies and how Western education researchers approach social situations. Its differences with Chinese philosophies were highlighted with the concept of *dao* and Confucianism. More than just an epistemological discussion, the author argues that some Western researchers' bias towards Asian researchers may be due to their failure or lack of experience in making the connections with Asian social systems. It attempts to provide some plausible explanations of the prevalence of bias by peer reviewers of Western journals.

Introduction

The plurality of research methodologies has given rise to much conflict between Western and Eastern researchers. There is a considerable amount of effort taken by researchers to apply the Western research approach to Eastern culture and traditions. The approach may not be effective as there are cultural differences between Western and Eastern societies. Researchers should develop culturally-competent research methodologies which are specific and valued by the cultures in which they operate.

Cultural competency is the core of many research programs. Researchers on Asian culture should not blindly accept those methodologies that are considered to be in compliance with Western standards as they may not fully answer the research questions according to the standards of Eastern culture. Asian researchers should be encouraged to challenge, rethink, and redevelop accepted forms of Western knowledge and theories within the local environment. The epistemological landscape in research is diverse and complex, researchers should be aware of the different research approaches and that there is no one standard methodology that is superior to the other as each approach has its limitations and relevance to the local culture.

Literature Review

Terre Blanche and Durrheim (1999) noted that the research process has three major dimensions: epistemology, ontology and methodology. Epistemological and ontological approaches refer to a person's perspective of the world. He could have either of the two possible perspectives: objectivistic or constructivist. His perception of the world may change depending on the situation. The research paradigm inherently reflects the researcher's beliefs and views of the world he lives in (Lather, 1986)

The two common epistemological philosophies adopted for social research are interpretivism and positivism (Galliers, 1991). The researcher's choice of research methods will depend on his experience and his perspective of the social world.

Interpretivists believe that reality is socially-constructed and that knowledge is derived from a variety of routes (Willis, 1995). Walsham (1995) argued that there are no correct or incorrect theories. Knowledge and meaning are results of interpretation (Gephart, 1999). Denzin (2010) noted that research efforts should be concerned with revealing multiple realities as opposed to searching for one objective reality. Interpretivist paradigm stresses the collection of information and interpreting the information collected. It is concerned with understanding the world through the subjective experiences of the researcher.

Interpretivism consists of two major philosophical branches: hermeneutics and phenomenology (Boland, 1985). Hermeneutics is a branch of interpretive philosophy which stressed that all human understanding is achieved by considering the interdependent meaning of parts and the whole they form (Klein and Myers, 1999).

Phenomenology focuses on individual experiences, beliefs and perceptions. It is concerned with the study of conscious experiences.

Smith *et al.* (2009) defined phenomenology as an approach to the study of experience and thinking in terms of the things that matter to our lives. Phenomenological research methods are widely used in qualitative studies where the researcher seeks to understand the subjects' experiences, behaviours and emotions.

Positivism is based on the ideas of French philosopher, August Comte. He emphasised that observation and reason are the best means of understanding human behaviour. Positivists believe that knowledge is objective and quantifiable. Objective reality is independent of the observer and that using the right research methods, the researcher can accurately capture that reality. They are interested in uncovering the truth through empirical means (Henning, Van Rensburg and Smith, 2004). Positivism regards humans as passive, controlled and determined by the external environment. Figure 1 shows the relationships between the two main branches of philosophies and research methodologies.

In Buddhism, the Three Universal Truths and the Four Noble Truths serve as the guiding principles for all Buddhists to follow. The first of the Three Universal Truths stressed that everything in life is impermanent and ever changing. The second universal truth is that since everything is changing, life based on possessions of things does not make one happy.

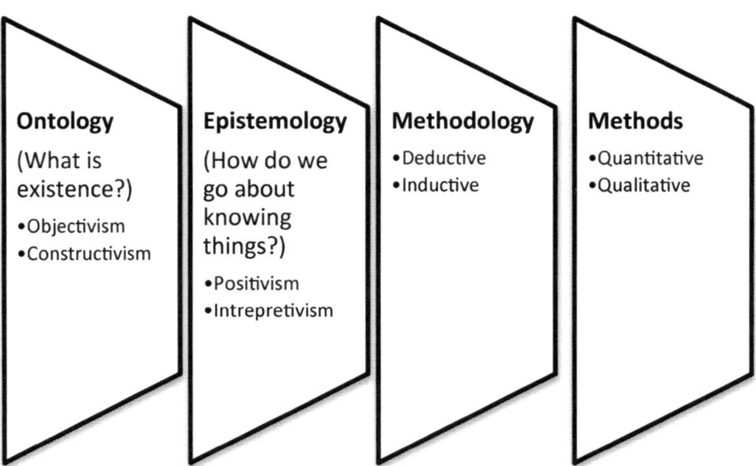

Fig. 1:   Two main branches of philosophies.

The third truth explained that continuous changes are due to the law of cause and effect.

Positivism has evolved and given rise to post-positivism. Post-positivists such as Patton (2002) reiterated that interpretations should be derived directly from data observed and collected. The limitation of post-positivism is that it assumes the researcher is able to observe and document reality objectively. This is a challenging task as the research process is influenced by the researcher's own cognitive predilections or past experiences.

Dutch sociologist, Geert Hofstede, recognised the importance of understanding a culture before working with it. Hofstede (2001) developed the Five Major Cultural Dimensions Model to study how values in the workplace are influenced by culture. His first construct of Power Distance Index (PDI) noted that all societies are unequal. Inequality and power are perceived from the followers. A high index indicates that hierarchy is clearly established while a low index indicates that people question authority. His findings showed that the PDI shows very high scores for Asian countries. Hofstede concept of understanding other cultures is in line with Confucianism constructs of harmony and non-confrontation (Chen, 2001; Knutson, Hwang, and Deng, 2000).

Buddhism advocates the practice of meditation as the means to transforming the mind. Buddhists look within themselves for truth and understanding of Buddha's teachings, Practitioners seek to cultivate the acceptance of everything so that there is no discrimination or internal struggle (Trungpa, 1996). In "The Four Noble Truths", the third truth of cessation deals with the possibility of giving up struggles to hold on to self-ego. In the fourth truth, known as "The Path", one has to learn to let go of the fixed sense of self-ego and self-centred constructions of others.

Bias

There are three main types of cognitive bias: prestige bias, conformity bias and confirmation bias. Bias is an intrinsic part of human nature and reviewers are not immune to exhibiting some form of bias when reviewing peer papers. In other words, the process of rejecting a peer paper may be due to bias rather than unsuitable submissions.

Prestige Bias — Prestige bias occurs when learners prefer to imitate models that are seen as having more prestige (Heinrich and Gil-White, 2001). It essentially capitalises on existing knowledge about who is worth mentioning. Richerson and Boyd (2005) noted that there are crucial differences between generic and cultural transmissions.

Buss and Duntley (2006) noted that individuals ascend the social hierarchy and attain influence by using manipulative and coercive means to increase his status or power. Other studies stressed that social hierarchy is determined entirely by social competence (Anderson and Kilduff, 2009). Cheng, *et al.* (2013) demonstrated that both dominance and prestige are viable strategies for ascending the social hierarchy.

Conformity Bias — Conformity bias notes that people conform strongly to behavioral norms. It is responsible for maintaining the differences between different cultures (Boyd and Richerson, 2005). Conformity may take either of two forms. When people rely on others to determine what is correct, it is referred as informational conformity. When they adjust their behaviors to fit in with the majority, it is known as normative conformity (Claidiere and Whiten, 2012). Social conformity serves as a buffer protecting individuals from negative pressures when outcomes become bad (Yu and Sun, 2013). Scientific dishonesty is common in the research community, in situations where authors deliberately comply with referees' instructions to get their papers published (Shibayama and Baba, 2016). The negative implication of dishonest publications is that it compromises the scientific knowledge base and deters the admission of new knowledge and findings.

Confirmation Bias — Confirmation bias or confirmatory bias occurs when people interpret or favour information that confirms their own beliefs, assumptions and preconceptions while giving less favourable consideration to alternative reasoning. This bias can lead to ignorance of new intellectual challenges or even discredit alternative learning solutions to a particular situation. As a result, literatures which may be methodologically sound may not be published as reviewers are prejudiced against the author with exhibit different research perspectives. People who support or oppose a particular issue will seek information that supports their beliefs and also interpret situations in a way that upholds their existing ideas. The negative implication of confirmatory bias in journal publications is quite serious and warrants further studies. Academicians often encounter cognitive bias in peer review processes from reviewers who may not share the same research philosophies as the reviewers. The lack of publication opportunities may deter a researcher's career advancement (Dixon, 1973). Mahoney (1977) found that reviewers were strongly biased against manuscripts that had results contrary to their theoretical perspectives. Confirmation bias challenges the impartiality of reviewers as they may evaluate submitted manuscripts based on their own theoretical and methodological preferences rather than the content of the literature (Lacey, 1999; Lee, 2009).

A number of related situations may spring to the forefront of the reviewers mind when doing a peer review. He may rely on previous information or events in making a judgment rather than focusing on the new event. This type of mental shortcut, known as availability heuristic, refers to a tendency to form a judgement on what readily comes to mind (Baumeister and Bushman, 2008).

When people with different views interpret information in a biased manner, their views and opinions move even further apart. This leads to biased assimilation and attitude polarisation. Highly opinionated people are likely to examine empirical evidence in a biased manner. Researchers lacking in cross-cultural experience often invalidate the results of researchers from another culture as they try to seek equivalence of familiar methodologies in the other cultures without fully understanding the context of the research problem.

The emic (culturally specific) approach investigates how behaviour of people is determined by local customs, meaning and beliefs (Kottak, 2006; Ager and Loughry, 2004). Behaviour is described in terms of cultural specificity and with internal criteria. The strength of the emic approach is that it allows the researcher to appreciate the uniqueness of the context being studied, in respect of the local cultures and beliefs.

On the other hand, the etic (culturally universal) approach describes culture in a way that is general and non-structural. The etic approach attempts to apply theories, perspectives and beliefs from outside of the setting being studied. The limitations of the etic approach is that it precludes the researcher to new approaches and concepts if he follows this approach blindly. Proponents of the etic approach appreciate the comparison across context and culture (Morris *et al.*, 1999).

Researchers need to possess two types of skills to be successful — theoretical and methodological skills. Theoretical skills are built up through years of experience, observation and reflection. These tacit skills cannot be taught but learned. On the other hand, methodological skills are relatively standard and relatively easily acquired through an academic programme.

Collectivism favours members of one's in-group and disfavours one's out-group (Leung and Stephan, 2001). East Asians seek to maintain harmony by resolving conflicts through compromises (Nisbett *et al.*, 2001). The hallmark of Confucianism is a balance between externalism and internalism, filial piety, grace and public service. Confucius uses rhetoric such as analogy and aphorism to relate his views. These methods may not be fully understood by Western thinkers who rely on deductive reasoning.

The Mahayana school of Buddhism stresses following Buddha's example of going out to the world and doing good. Mahayana Buddhism encourages everyone to embark on Bodhisattvas. The term essentially refers to someone on the path to Awakening and calls on Buddhists to enlighten themselves as well as enlightening others.

Daoism, another Chinese philosophical and religious tradition, focuses on the relationship between humanity and ever-changing cosmos; health and longevity; and the concept of *wu-wei* (non-action). Daoist ideas and teachings were recorded in texts such as Daodejing, Zhuangzhi and Huainanzi. Dao is regarded as the metaphysical source of all that exists throughout the universe and across three temporalities: the past, the present and the future.

A comparative study of educational research by Zhao *et al.* (2008) found that Chinese researchers focus more on macro issues that have greater implications on the education reform and policies of China. American professors, on the contrary, are more interested in micro issues. The differences may be partly due to the epistemological differences between the two countries. Traditionally, Chinese focus on more on holistic issues while Americans are more inclined towards analytical tradition (Nisbett, 2003). Chinese researchers are more likely to conduct qualitative studies than quantitative research. This is not surprising as Chinese epistemological teaching is based on a holistic world view and relational in all aspects (Rosker, 2012). Chinese believe that the external world is orderly structured and the human mind is also structured in accordance to the cosmic order. Metaphysics are a central concept of Chinese philosophy and their origin could be traced back to The Book of Changes (Yijing). Many Western researchers argued that metaphysics are purely speculative, not empirically based and not verifiable. Chinese philosophers labelled the ultimate reality as *Dao* (the "way") and regarded the fundamental operating principle of the world as the balancing of forces known as Yin-Yang. Yu and Xu (2009) argued that the Chinese philosophy of *Dao* is "metaphysics of ethics" and stresses morality and emotion but ignores reason.

Leung (2009) argued that non-Western researchers are able to develop novel ideas and theories that are applicable to Western cultures. They have the potential to contribute to universal theories by modifying Western concepts and by offering brand new theories (Li *et al.*, 2012). While many scholars tend to characterise Chinese theories as having a relational and collectivistic orientation and Western knowledge as largely self-focused, Triandis (1996) noted that both collective and individualistic tendencies are present in any given culture. This is in contrast to Hofstede concept that culture is relatively homogenous (1980).

Egalitarianism is fast gaining momentum as Asian universities seek to be treated the same as their Western counterparts. The core of the egalitarian idea is to treat people as equals (Dworkin, 2000). This desire to gain equality has led researchers at Shanghai Jiao Tong University to develop the Academic Ranking of World Universities (ARWU) standard which competes with Western universities ranking measures such as the QS World University Rankings and Times Higher University Rankings. As the Chinese government invests heavily in universities such as Peking, Tsinghua and Fudan to rival Western universities in the areas of research and development, it is determined to set its own standards of university ranking rather than being dictated by the two Western ranking publications. In the 2015 Academic Ranking of World Universities, seven Chinese universities made it to the top 200. Conversely, only Peking and Tsinghua universities made it to the top 200 in the Times Higher World University Rankings 2015–2016.

Discussion

If a research methodology is not aligned with the culture, the effectiveness of the new strategy is questionable. Western researchers have to be aware that applying Western models or methodologies without taking into consideration their experiences in the culture will only lead to research bias, a bias produced by cultural dependency rather than the research methodology itself. Western research methodologies are social constructs and developed according to the interests and tastes of the researchers in the West. The problem of social construction has become evident in different constructions of culture and arises from the historical dominance of Western perspectives in the field of social sciences. This lack of diverse and non-Western perspectives tends to develop scholars who are narrow in their perspectives of other cultures. Universities in the West need to have a pool of academicians which are able to reflect the diversity of experiences in other cultures. One probable reason could be that the acceptance of authoritative structure in Asian countries as reflected in the high Power Distance Index as found in Hofstede studies. The perception that Western research methodology is the standard or norm for social research studies has coerced many researchers to align themselves to Western methods instead of embracing alternative but more culturally relevant research methods.

Western and Eastern philosophers perceive the world quite differently. Western philosophers' thoughts were largely analytical, focusing on formal logic. Chinese thoughts, on the other hand, were holistic, seeking to understand the relationships among objects and events in the field. They are more likely to propose "middle way" solutions between contradictory propositions. While ancient Western philosophers saw stability in the world, Chinese scholars saw change, in line with *yin* and *yang* of the *Dao*.

Asian researchers should challenge, rethink and redevelop accepted forms of Western knowledge that are broadly located within social sciences and reexamine their applicability to Eastern cultural context. The issue of methodological commensurability involves comparison of traditions and cultures. The imposition of one's values and beliefs onto others will likely result in ethnocentrism and conflicts. Ethnocentrism is prevalent in peer reviews as reviewers often prematurely judge other researchers in relation to their own culture, language and beliefs (Kuzban *et al.*, 2001). It hinders cooperation and communication with other groups and presents a myopic view of one's beliefs. Alford *et al.* (2005) suggested that a number of political beliefs and behaviours may be influenced by heritable tendencies that are results from evolution. The human mind is predisposed to think and react in a certain way (Brown, 2004; Wrangham, 2004).

Critics of ethnocentrism support the concept of cultural relativism which stress that all norms, beliefs and values are dependent on their cultural context and should be treated as such. It is the author's view that no culture is superior to another culture when comparing systems of morality, law, politics, etc. The behaviour of one culture should not be judged by the standards of another culture. Relativists believe that all truth is relative and that there are no absolute truths. Conflicts will be minimised when one respect the values and standards of a different culture. Researchers should recognise that they do not fully understand the other cultures and that they may be assuming something that is out of context when conducting research studies of different cultures. This is evident from Hofstede *Confucian Dynamism* which did not support one of the five dimensions of cultural factors — *Predictability (Uncertainty Avoidance)*. In Chinese culture, there is a general perseverance in pursuing a goal and that hierarchies are carefully observed (Hofstede and Bond, 1998).

In Buddhism, a verse from the Goddess of Mercy Mantra "Gods in Heaven, Gods on Earth, humans apart from disaster, disaster apart from bodies, all misfortune turn into dust". A broad interpretation of "misfortune" could be "worries". Applying this broad Buddhist concept to research methodology, researchers who fail to comprehend new thoughts and fail to see through new ideas will have difficulties comprehending new perspectives of social situations. Different thoughts or actions may create different learning outcomes. The development of wisdom and the nurturing of the mind form the philosophical basis of Buddhism perspective on education. The possibility of self-transformation through mental development will enable one to have a better understanding of the true nature of reality.

Because prestige bias is cultural specific, a generalisation across other cultures leads to discriminatory assessments about the latter's learning strategies. Practitioners of Western cultural systems often attempt to subvert the learning models of other cultures. The differences between Western and Eastern learning models could be traced to philosophical differences of the West and East. Prestige and dominance are highly intertwined. The association with a dominant culture makes a practitioner feels that he is in a prestigious position. Likewise, the association with a prestigious environment promotes the feeling of dominance over others. Such interlocking behaviours often give rise to self-perceived superiority over others and forms the core of human hierarchical relationships. This relationship is illustrated in Fig. 2.

Individuals ascend up the social hierarchy and attain influence by using manipulative and coercive means to increase his status or power (Buss and Duntley, 2006). Other studies stressed that social hierarchy is determined entirely by social competence (Anderson and Kilduff, 2009). Cheng *et al.* (2013) demonstrated that both dominance and prestige are viable strategies for ascending the social hierarchy. This perception have prompted some Eastern scholars to rethink the adaptability of Western research methodologies to Asian cultures.

What things are prestigious are often determined by the culture, social class or group membership. It is, thus, not too surprising to expect that that most academicians in the East will have their works published in journals from the East. The degree or extent of how much biases in peer review is difficult to quantify as there are inconsistencies in peer assessments between countries or types of journals. As peer reviewers are often contemporaries or competitors of the researcher, there is a high possibility

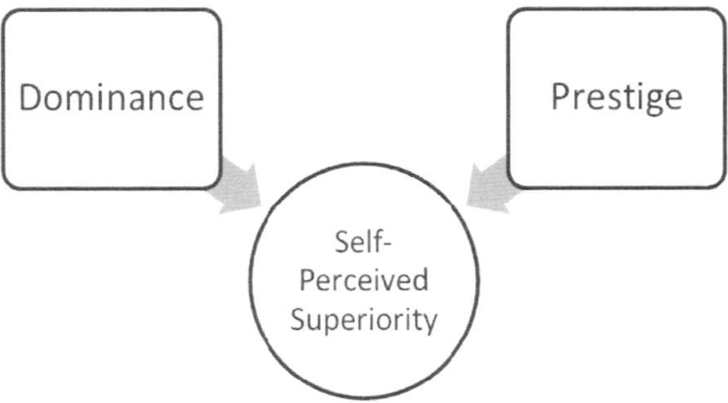

Fig. 2:   Self-perceived superiority.

Fig. 3:   Heuristics of reviewer.

that they tend to give less-favourable results to the author due to selfish reasons. In reality, competition for research funding is a powerful tool to discredit a peer's research paper.

Figure 3 shows the heuristics of peer reviewers as two opposing forces within an individual. At one end, the "ideal self" seeks to be an ideal person demonstrating the characteristics of objectivity and non-bias. At the other end, the "real self" is an individual with entrenched beliefs, selfish motives, insecure and fearing competition. This cognitive dissonance within an individual has a powerful influence on the individual's behaviour and actions. To release the tension, the individual may justify his behaviour by either focusing on more supportive beliefs that outweigh the dissonant behaviour or reduce the importance of the conflicting belief (Festinger, 1964). Applying the theory of cognitive dissonance to peer reviewers, we can speculate that some reviewers attempt to justify their actions by decreasing the importance of the dissonant cognition (that there is no ideal self in a person).

Conclusion

Western researchers have often criticised that Confucianism fails to provide the rights of individuals that may have conflict with the community. They argued that Eastern cultures suppress dissenters who attempt to highlight power abuses by authorities. In a broader sense, this seems contradictory as some Western researchers seek to impose their beliefs on Asian researchers in peer review articles. They seek to ignore or downplay alternative views and opinions of Asian researchers indicating faults in their research methodologies. These incidents highlighted the myopic views of some Western researchers who do not fully understand the background of Asian culture. The Analects of Confucius maintained that "in teachings, there should be no distinction of classes". Similarly, there should be no distinction in terms of superiority or inferiority as far as knowledge, culture, experiences and beliefs are concerned. Each culture emphasises different values and there should be no judgement of superiority. On one hand, some Western researchers advocate the rights of dissenters to voice their views, but on the other hand, they fail to acknowledge that there are differences in their philosophical views with Asian researchers. Comparative philosophy focuses on understanding of historical developments, similarities and dissimilarities between different cultures or ethnic groups. Different social systems will adopt different approaches and methodologies to the subject of study. Rather than viewing Asian researchers from a Western perspective, Western and Eastern researchers should learn from each other and jointly collaborate on research studies or topics of philosophical significance. This conclusion is anecdotal rather than empirical as any comparative research on this topic will likely be mired with bias of the researchers. The cultural complexities across borders makes it an even more challenging tasks to conduct education research objectively for the research design and methodologies in themselves will display elements of bias due to the predilections, beliefs and experiences of the researchers.

References

Alford, J.R., Funk, C.L. and Hibbing, J.R. (2005). Are political orientations genetically transmitted? *American Political Science Review,* **99**(2), 153–167.

Anderson, C., and Kilduff, G.J. (2009). The pursuit of status in social groups. *Current Directions in Psychological Science,* **18**(5), 295–298.

Baumeister, R.F., and Bushman, B.J. (2008). *Social Psychology and Human Nature.* San Francisco, CA: Wadsworth.

Boland, R.J. (1985). Phenomenology: a preferred approach to research on information systems. In: *Research Methods in Information Systems,* Mumford E.,

Hirschheim, R.A., Fitzgerald, G., and WoodHarper T. (Eds.), pp. 193–201, Elsevier Science Publishers B.V., North-Holland.

Brown, D.E. (2004). Human universals, human nature, and human culture. *Daedalus*, **133**(4), 47–54.

Buss, D.M., and Duntley, J.D. (2006). The evolution of aggression. In: Schaller, M., Simpson, J.A., and Kenrick, D.T. (Eds.), *Evolution and social psychology* (pp. 263–286). New York Psychology Press.

Chen, G.M. (2001). Toward transcultural understanding: A harmony theory of Chinese communication. In Milhouse, V.H., Asante, M.K., and Nwosu, P.O. (Eds.), *Transcultural realities: Interdisciplinary perspectives on cross-cultural relations* (pp. 55–70). Thousand Oaks: SAGE.

Cheng, J.T., Tracy, J.L., Foulsham, T., Kingstone, A., and Heinrich, J. (2013). Two ways to the top: Evidence that dominance and prestige are distinct yet viable avenues to social rank and influence. *Journal of Personality and Social Psychology*, **104**(1), 103–125.

Claidiere, N., and Whiten, A. (2012). Integrating the study of conformity and culture in humans and nonhuman animals. *Psychological Bulletin*, **138**, 126–145. doi: 10.1037/a0025868.

Denzin, N.K. (2010). *The qualitative manifesto: A call to arms.* Walnut Creek, CA: Left Coast Press.

Dixon, B. (1973). *What is Science for?* New York: Harper & Row.

Dworkin, R. (2000). *Sovereign Virtue: Equality in Theory and Practice*, Cambridge: Harvard University Press.

Festinger, L. (Ed.) (1964). *Conflict, decision, and dissonance* (Vol. 3). Stanford University Press.

Galliers, R.D. (1991). Strategic information systems planning: myths, reality and guidelines for successful implementation. *European Journal of Information Systems*, **1**(1), 55–64.

Gephart, R. (1999). Paradigms and research methods. Research Methods Forum, 4(Summer), Retrieved October 3, 2009 from the Academy of Management website, http://division.aomonline.org/rm/1999_RMD_Forum_Paradigms_and_Research_Methods.htm.

Heinrich, J., and Gil-White, F.J. (2001). The evolution of prestige. Freely conferred deference as a mechanism for enhancing the benefits of cultural transmission. *Evolution and Human Behaviour*, **22**, 165–196.

Henning, E., Van Rensburg, W., and Smit, B. (2004). *Finding your way in Qualitative Research.* Van Schaik: Pretoria.

Hofstede, G. (1980). *Culture's Consequences: International differences in work-related values.* Beverly Hills, CA, and London: SAGE.

Hofstede, G., and Bond, M.H. (1998). The Confucius Connection: From cultural roots to economic growth, *Organisational Dynamics, Spring*, 1998, pp. 5–21.

Hofstede, G. (2001). *Culture's Consequences, Comparing Values, Behaviors, Institutions and Organizations Across Nations,* 2nd edn., SAGE, Thousand Oaks.

Klein, H.K., and Myers, M.D. (1999). A Set of Principles for Conducting and Evaluating Interpretive Field Studies in Information Systems, *MIS Quarterly,* **23**(1), 67–93.

Knutson, T.J., Hwang, J.C., and Deng, B.C. (2000). Perception and management of conflict: A comparison of Taiwanese and US business employees. *Intercultural Communication Studies,* **9**, 1–32.

Kottak, C. (2006). *Mirror for Humanity,* New York, NY: McGraw Hill, ISBN 978-0-07-803490-9.

Kurzban, R., Tooby, J., & Cosmides, L. (2001). Can race be erased? Coalitional computation and social categorization. *Proceedings of the National Academy of Science, USA,* **98**(26), 15387–15392.

Lacey, H. (1999). *Is science value free? Values and scientific understanding.* New York: Routledge.

Lather, P. (1986). Research as Praxis. *Harvard Educational Review,* **56**(3), 257–277.

Lee, C.J., Sugimoto, C.R., Zhang, G., & Cronin, B. (2013). Bias in Peer Review. *Journal of the American Society for Information Science and Technology,* **64**(1), 2–17.

Leung, K., & Stephan, W. (2001). Social justice from a cultural perspective. In Matsumoto, D. (Ed.). *Handbook of culture and psychology* (pp. 375–410). New York: Oxford University Press.

Leung, K. (2009). Never the twain shall meet? Integrating Chinese and Western management research. *Management and Organization Review,* **5**, 121–129.

Li, P.P., Leung, K., Chen, C.C., and Luo, J.D. (2012). Indigenous research on Chinese management: What and how. *Management and Organization Review,* **8**, 7–24.

Mahoney, M.J. (1997). Publication Prejudices: An Experimental Study of Confirmatory Bias in the Peer Review System. *Cognitive Therapy and Research,* **1**(2), 161–175.

Morris, M.W., Leung, K., Ames, D., and Lickel, B. (January 01, 1999). Views from inside and outside: Integrating Emic and Etic Insights about Culture and Justice Judgment. *Academy of Management Review,* **24**(4), 781–796.

Nisbett, R., Peng, K., Choi, I., and Norenzayan, A. (2001). Culture systems of thought: Holistic versus analytical cognition. *Psychological Review,* **108**, 291–310.

Nisbett, R.E. (2003). *The Geography of Thought: How Asians and Westerners Think Differently, and Why.* Free Press, New York.

Patton, M.Q. (2002). *Qualitative research & evaluation methods.* Thousand Oaks, CA: SAGE Publications.

Ray, R.A. (2000). *Indestructable truth.* Boston & London: Shambhala Publications.

Richerson, P.J., and Boyd, R. (2005). *Not by Genes Alone: How Culture Transformed Human Evolution.* Chicago: University of Chicago Press.

Rošker, J.S. (2012). "Traditional Chinese Epistemology: The Structural Compatibility of Mind and External World", Zheng da Zhong wen xue bao, **17**, 1–16.

Shibayama, S., and Baba, Y. (2016). Dishonest Conformity in Peer Review. *Prometheus* (forthcoming).

Smith, J., Flowers, P., and Larkin, M. (2009). *Interpretive phenomenological analysis: Theory, method and research.* Thousand Oaks, CA: SAGE.

Terre Blanche, M., and Durrheim, K. (1999). *Research in practice.* Cape Town: UCT Press.

Triandis, H.C. (1996). The psychological measurement of cultural syndromes. *American Psychologist*, **51**, 407–415.

Trungpa, C. (1996). *Meditation in Action.* London and Boston: Shambhala Publications.

Walsham, G. (1995). Interpretive case studies in IS research: nature and method. *European Journal of Information Systems*, **4**(2), 74–81.

Walsham, G. (2005). Doing Interpretive Research. *European Journal of Information System*, 15, 320–330.

Willis, J. (1995). A recursive, reflective instructional design model based on constructivist-interpretist theory. *Educational Technology*, **35**(6), 5–23.

Wrangham, R. (2004). Killer species. *Daedalus*, **133**(4), 25–35.

Zhao, Y., Zhang, G., Yang, W., Kirkland, D., Han. X., and Zhang, J. (2008). A comparative study of educational research in China and the United States. *Asia Pacific Journal of Education*, **28**(1), 1–17.

Yu, R., and Sun, S. (2013). To Conform or Not to Conform: Spontaneous Conformity Diminishes the Sensitivity to Monetary Outcomes. *PLOS ONE* 8(5):e64530.doi:10.1371/journal.pone.0064530.

Yu, W., and Xu, J. (2009). "Morality and Nature: The Essential Difference between the Dao of Chinese Philosophy and the Metaphysics in Western Philosophy", *Frontiers of Philosophy in China*, **4**(3), 360–366.

學而時習之, 不亦悅乎?

To learn and to practise what is learned time and again is pleasure, is it not?

Analects of Confucius

Chapter 2

Readdressing Key Challenges Facing Higher Education Institutions

This chapter explores the complexities of multiple paradigms and overlapping influences in university leadership today. The perceptions of the key issues and challenges facing higher education leaders in their work are discussed. The study found that many challenges centred around the need for strategic leadership, flexibility, autonomy, managing and motivating staff, responding to competing tensions and maintaining institutional quality. The author also comes up with some proposals for university leaders to deal with the challenges they face.

Introduction

This section explores the complexities of multiple paradigms and overlapping influences in higher education leadership today. It commences with a review of literature relating to issues and challenges in higher education leadership. The second section outlines the findings from participants about their perceptions of the university leadership. The final section of the paper provides some implications of this study for the higher education sector.

Much research has been done on competing challenges impacting academic staff and administrators. The goal of the university is to offer quality higher education experience to students and to fulfil the needs of society (Longden, 2006). University leaders may, however, focus on competing paradigms such as "student as scholars" versus "students as consumers". Snyder *et al.* (2007) and Giroux (2005) noted the interactive forces of mass education and of sound pedagogical principles in university education.

University leaders have different views on delivering education based on sound principles of pedagogy and the need to create efficiencies of mass education (Coaldrake and Stedman, 1999; Meek and Wood, 1997; Pratt and Poole, 1999; Ramsden, 1998; Szekeres, 2006). In the United Kingdom, higher education providers have opted for either larger classes or reduced contact time, or a combination of both due to resource reduction (Longden, 2006).

Stiles (2004) and Whitchurch (2006) pointed to the challenges for academics to partner with industries and government to compete for industry-based funding and undertake research and development. The academic has to interact with the various parties to synthesise academic and business agendas (Whitchurch, 2006).

In today's competitive environment, leaders need to have the courage to take action when the future remains unclear (Barnett, 2004) and Hanna (2003). The capacity to support and develop leaders capable of handling complex issues and engaging people effectively and leading through changes is a strategic necessity for today's higher education institutions (Fulmer, Gibbs and Goldsmith, 2005).

Methodology

This qualitative study investigates the perceptions of mid to senior level executives of a Malaysian private university college on what were they see as the main issues and challenges facing them today. A total of 15 executives, ranging from Head of Schools and departmental heads to faculty administration managers, participated in the interviews. Open-ended questions were posed as they provided the opportunity for the participants to express their views. This methodology, where interviews were normally held in informal settings where participants felt comfortable to provide their views is the most effective method in qualitative research (Silverman, 2000).

Each participant was asked the same set of questions with flexibility to explore issues that may surface during the interview (Merriam, 1998).

The advantage of this type of interview is that they reduce interviewer bias during the interview and facilitation of organisation and analysis of data (Fraenkel and Wallen, 2003). The interview protocols consisted of ten semi-structured, open-ended questions in the endeavour to gain insights into the participants' perceptions on leadership practices:

(1) How do you assess the university college climate?
(2) How much academic freedom exists in the university college?
(3) What do you think should be done to maintain academic quality?
(4) Are staff generally satisfied with their jobs and remuneration?
(5) How concerned is the leadership team about staff welfare?
(6) How effective is the leadership team?
(7) What do you think are the main causes of stress in your work?
(8) How responsive is the leadership to change?
(9) Does the leadership team makes an effort to treat others with trust and respect?
(10) How serious is the leadership team in their beliefs to encourage others to improve their skills and abilities?

Findings and Discussion

The study found four key issues and challenges facing university leaders today. These are:

(1) Ensuring academic freedom.
(2) Maintaining staff motivation.
(3) Maintaining institutional quality.
(4) Providing effective leadership.

Ensuring academic freedom

Academic freedom is defined as right to speak freely without fear of reprisal, the right to determine specific teaching methodologies, the right to transmit knowledge openly, and the right to research in one's field.

Barnett (1990) argued that academic freedom should be expanded from its narrow definition of staff immunity from censorship towards a universal mandate to present and to criticise ideas. Fessel (2006) urged universities to issue clear statements affirming their commitment to academic freedom and controversial debate.

Developing trust in all relationships is essential for universities leadership to be successful. Trust provides the environment to motivate people to act and collaborate. Trust and power are closely interrelated. Power without trust destroys its own basis, while trust without power is not sustainable because there always will be the potential for conflict in a group. A good university leader must be endowed with appropriate means of power and be able to earn trust from his subordinates.

The study found that many participants remained timid and reserved expressing their opinions to the university leaders as they felt that their views would not be appreciated. Repression of ideas and opinions by top management came in the form of threats of dismissal or questioning the competency of the staff to handle a particular task. The fear of unfair discrimination by university leaders have discouraged many participants to discuss openly important subject matters which could promote critical thinking about controversial ideas. University leaders should treat everyone with respect and encourage an open, honest and constructive environment for discussion to take place.

The United Nations Educational, Scientific and Cultural Organization and the International Labour Organization issued the statement: "The principle of academic freedom should be scrupulously observed. Higher education teaching personnel are entitled to the maintaining of academic freedom, that is to say, the right, without constriction by prescribed doctrine, to freedom of teaching and discussion, freedom in carrying out research and disseminating and publishing the results thereof, freedom to express freely their opinion about the institution or system in which they work, freedom from institutional censorship and freedom to participate in professional or representative academic bodies. All higher education teaching personnel should have the right to fulfil their functions without discrimination of any kind and without fear of repression by the state or any other source".

Universities should adopt clear policies supporting academic freedom and steps to deal with challenges to academic freedom in order to support higher-order thinking across the campus. Academics should be encouraged to promote critical thinking without fear of reprisals from university leaders.

Maintaining staff motivation

Maslow's (1954) needs theory raised the question as to whether people's needs would be met by choosing careers which related to job satisfaction. The absence of three higher-order needs (self-esteem, autonomy, and self-actualisation) were shown to be a major contributor to low teacher satisfaction (Carver and Sergiovanni, 1971; Frances and Lebras, 1982; Sweeney, 1981; Trusty and Sergiovanni, 1966; Wright, 1985).

Bandura's (1997) self-efficacy theory relates to whether people believe they can be successful in their chosen careers and the number of career alternatives that they may consider. He suggested that self-efficacy influences performance, behavioural choices, and persistence and is related to career choice in a number of ways. Self-efficacy complements skill sets in individuals seeking careers and may facilitate career attainment for those seeking careers in areas that they are competent in.

Research has shown that a positive school culture was associated with increased student motivation and achievement, improved teacher collaboration, and improved attitudes among teachers toward their jobs (Sashkin and Sashkin, 1990; Sashkin and Wahlberg, 1993; Ogawa and Bossert, 1995). Teachers are transformational leaders and they may also influence students performance if they are motivated themselves.

Other research indicated that the higher the expected importance or value of present activities is in relation to future personal goals, the higher the motivation of individuals and the better their performance and learning (Raynor, 1974).

The study revealed that participants considered three main drivers of motivation. The first is the ability to make a difference in other people's lives. This include imparting their knowledge to students. The self-efficacy theory of Bandura is centrally relevant to their beliefs in their capacity to successfully carried out their given tasks and the consequent impact this belief has on their motivation.

The second area is their working environment whereby they felt that their contribution will be appreciated. This include opportunities for career advancement as well as personal growth. Rowe and Rowe (1999) found that teacher professional development has the potential for enhancing the educational outcomes of students and assisting teachers to operate more effectively in the classroom.

The remaining area relates to salary and benefits. While they are altruistic in nature, a low compensation package would lower their motivation and even prompt them to seek alternative employment elsewhere. All participants regard salary level and welfare conditions as a factors affecting their job satisfaction. However, it is also intertwined with other factors such as university leadership, professional development and a sense of achievement through teaching.

Maintaining institutional quality

The quality management system in a higher education institution focuses on quality assurance and self-assessment at all levels according to the standards set up by the respective educational authorities. The implementation of the quality management system involves both an internal institutional development as well as an external one in which certain mechanism of control can assure the quality of the educational process. The quality assurance and enhancement processes have to contain the following elements (Fig. 1):

(a) Transparency
(b) Accountability
(c) Institutional Self-Awareness
(d) Information Gathering
(e) Development and Monitoring

The development of a culture of organisational excellence could be categorized into eight major themes, according to the European Foundation for Quality Management (EFQM) framework. These are:

(a) Leadership
(b) Policy and Strategy
(c) Staff Management

Fig. 1:   Quality assurance framework.

(d) Resources
(e) Key Process Management
(f) Financial Result
(g) Customer Satisfaction
(h) Staff Satisfaction
(i) Impact on Society

Leadership reflects the attitudes and resolutions in which university leaders choose to sustain excellence. They have to set clearly defined policies and strategies to reflect the set of objectives and the means to achieve those strategies. The implementation of a quality assurance system poses much challenge since it requires a change in the work culture at all levels.

While the approach to quality assurance is in the right direction, the study revealed that participants felt that there were many underlying issues which require attention. These include:

(a) University leaders not actively listening to staff ideas and feedback. Rewarding staff for their good work and providing feedback to them will contribute to the positive working environment. The delegation of prerogatives within faculties and departments is essential when it comes to teaching and research. If academic freedom is not protected or being suppressed, the notion of a university will disappear.

(b) Implementing a professional development plan for staff is an important working condition. The professional development plan should be a conscious and serious initiative. To be meaningful, staff participation is encouraged to determine the content of the plan.

(c) Many participants felt that there is a need to balance competing demands such as increasing student enrolment and maintaining academic quality. Raising the entry requirements of students will result in lower enrolment numbers initially. University leaders need to avoid two different direction-setting practices which influence stress levels of subordinates. The lack of transparency and the absence of useful information concerning academic activities contributed to low performance. Determining, then implementing the appropriate strategy, putting in place the organisational structure and developing conducive organisational culture present major challenges for university leaders. Barnett (1992) advised that senior staff can employ and encourage the more subtle "two i" approach of inform and involve rather than the army-style "two c" approach of command and control.

(d) Participants revealed the competing tensions around research and teaching, enrolment numbers and quality, and administration and academic work. Gayle *et al.* (2003) suggested that there are implicit tensions of managing universities in a business-like way. The challenge for universities leaders is to identify a sustainable collaborative model which balances the needs of administrative demands and academic quality.

Providing effective leadership

The assessment and evaluation of the effectiveness of a university leader is more than just his knowledge of finance, strategic planning or curriculum development. In the corporate environment, an effective leader is measured by his performance in bringing the company to profitability and maximising the return on investment (ROI). In an educational setting, the emphasis on the development of dispositions to motivate the application of knowledge and skills, and technical expertise is of equal importance. Dispositions are defined by Perkins (1995) as proclivities that motivate and determine the direction of behaviour.

The work of Goleman (1998) in the area of emotional intelligence focused on assessment and evaluation of leader behaviours not related to technical skills in the areas of finance, curriculum development, or strategic planning. Emotional intelligence is defined as the awareness of emotions and using emotions to make good decisions. Emotional intelligence involves empathy, managing emotions in relations, and persuading others (O'Neil, 1996). Coleman (1998) and Salopek (1998) stated that competencies associated with emotional intelligence are more important in effective job performance than are ability and expertise. To be a successful leader, the individual needs to possess a high level of emotional competencies.

From the study, the participants did not question the technical competencies and cognitive abilities of the university leaders. However, they remained unconvinced about the leaders' emotional competencies. The lack of trust in subordinates, the inability to keep emotions under control, the lack of empathy, the failure to proactively understand and meet other's needs and the difficulty to inspire others were some issues highlighted during the interviews. University leaders should find strategies to work through these situations if they are to earn the respect and trust of their colleagues.

Implications and Conclusion

The study revealed the need for university leaders to acknowledge the human dimension in the process of achieving their corporate goals. They need to be able to engage staff to embrace strategic change rather than focusing on the structure itself. The study reflects the importance of getting individuals involved in accomplishing specific tasks. Leaders need to be able to enter into an honest dialogue with the team members and be willing to hear different opinions on all issues. The findings revealed that it is essential for university leaders to work to develop the positive people skills and necessary communication skills to maintain the respect and treatment that members of the organisation deserve.

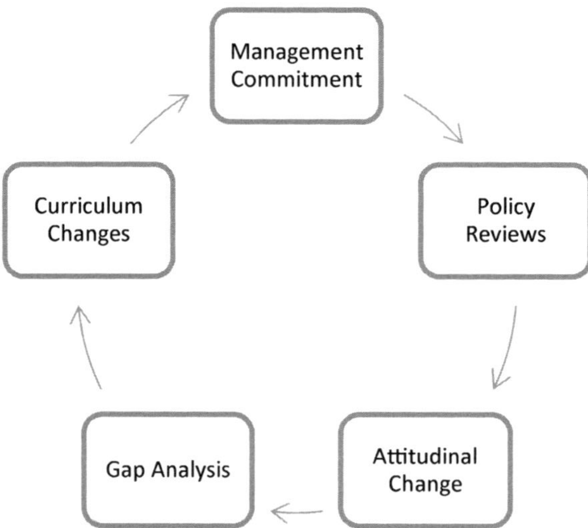

Fig. 2: Quality enhancement transformation process.

Participants indicated that continuous improvement could only be achieved in an environment where leaders are open to hearing their opinions. Organisational learning experience will be restricted unless there is a way of sharing the insights gained. Universities need to pay close attention to the tenets of leadership and selecting candidates based on their beliefs, skills and knowledge regarding the process of improving the educational institution. The quality enhancement transformation process requires commitment from top management as well as attitudinal changes from faculty and staff (Fig. 2).

Limitations

The main limitation of this study is the small sample size. The second limitation is whether the sample size may have been unduly unfavourable given that four participants have left the university college to join other educational institutions. Their opinion may be negatively biased against the university's top leadership team.

Literature on the topic of emotional competencies is quite limited. More research needs be conducted on this important topic with regards to improving the leadership of educational institutions today. The limitations of the existing research on emotional competencies could be due to the difficulty of establishing research settings which will enable us to further our comprehension of this topic.

References

Bandura, A. (1997). *Self-efficacy: The exercise of control*. New York: W.H. Freeman.

Barnett, R. (1990). *The Idea of Higher Education*. Buckingham, UK: Open University Press.

Barnett, R. (1992). *Improving Higher Education*. Buckingham: SHRE/Open University Press.

Barnett, R. (2004). Learning for an unknown future. *Higher Education Research & Development*, **23**(3), 247–260.

Carver, F.D., and Sergiovanni, T.J. (1971). Complexity, adaptability, and job satisfaction in high schools: An axiomatic theory applied. *Journal of Educational Administration*, **9**(1), 10–31.

Coaldrake, P., and Stedman, L. (1999). *Academic work in the twenty-first century: Changing roles and policies*. Occasional Papers Series (pp. 1–35). Canberra: Australian Department of Education, Training and Youth Affairs.

Dreschel, B., Prenzel, M., and Kramer, K. (2001, April). *How teachers perceive motivation in vocational education classrooms: An intervention study*. Paper presented at the annual meeting of the American Educational Research Association, Seattle, WA.

Fessel, S. (2006). The impact of academic freedom policies on critical thinking instruction. *Insight: A Collection of Faculty Scholarship*, **1**, 51–58.

Frances, R., and Lebras, C. (1982). The prediction of job satisfaction. *International Review of Applied Psychology*, **31**, 391–410.

Frankel, J.R., and Wallen, N.E. (2003). *How to design and evaluate research in education*. Boston, MA. McGraw-Hill.

Fulmer, R.M., Gibbs, P.A., and Goldsmith, M. (2000). Developing leaders: How winning companies keep on winning. *Sloan Management Review*, Fall, pp. 49–59.

Giroux, H. (2005). Academic entrepreneurs: The corporate takeover of higher education. *Tikkum*, **20**(2), 18–22.

Goleman, D. (1998). *Working with emotional intelligence*. New York: Bantam Books.

Hanna, D.E. (2003). Building a leadership vision: Eleven strategic challenges for higher education. *Educause*, July–August, pp. 25–34.

Hidi, S., and Renninger, K.A. (2006). The four-phase model of interest development. *Educational Psychologist*, **41**, 111–127.

Knight, P.T., and Trowler, P.R. (2000). Department level cultures and the improvement of learning and teaching. *Studies in Higher Education, 25,* 69–83.

Long, J.F., and Murphy, P.K. (2005, April). *Connecting through the content: The responsiveness of teacher and student interest in a required course.* Paper presented at the annual meeting of the American Educational Research Association, Montreal.

Long, J., and Woolfolk Hoy, A. (2006). Interested instructors: A composite portrait of individual differences and effectiveness. *Teaching and Teacher Education, 22,* 303–314.

Longden, B. (2006). An institutional response to changing student expectations and their impact on retention rates. *Journal of Higher Education Policy and Management, 28*(2), 173–187.

Maslow, A.H. (1954). *Motivation and personality.* New York: Harper & Brothers.

Meek, V.L., and Wood, F.Q. (1997). *Higher education government and management: An Australian study.* Evaluations and Investigations Program, Higher Education Division, Department of Employment, Education, Training and Youth Affairs. January. Retrieved September 13, 2003, from http://www.detya.gov.au/archive/highered/eippubs/eip9701/front.htm.

Merriam, S.B. (1998). *Qualitative research and case study applications in education.* San Francisco, CA: Josey-Bass.

O'Neil, J. (1996). On emotional intelligence: A conversation with Daniel Goleman, *Educational Leadership, 54*(1), 6–11.

Ogawa, R., and Bossert, S. (1995). Leadership as an organizational quality. *Educational Administration Quarterly, 31,* 224–243.

Perkins, D. (1995). Outsmarting I.Q: *The emerging science of learnable intelligence.* New York: The Free Press.

Pratt, G., and Poole, D. (1999). Globalisation and Australian universities, policies and impacts. *International Journal of Public Sector Management, 12*(6), 533–544.

Ramsden, P. (1998). Managing the Effective University. *Higher Education Research and Development, 17*(3), 347–370.

Raynor, J.O. (1974) Relationships between achievement-related motives, future orientation, and academic performances. In: Atkinson J.W. and Taynor J.O. (Eds.) *Motivation and Achievement,* pp. 121–154 (Washington DC, Winston).

Rowe, K.J., and Rowe, K.S. (1999). Investigating the relationship between students' attentive-inattentive behaviors in the classroom and their literacy progress. *International Journal of Educational Research, 31,* 1–138.

Sashkin, M., and Sashkin, M. (1990). *Leadership and culture building in schools: Quantitative and qualitative understandings.* Paper presented at the annual meeting of the American Educational Research Association, Boston, MA.

Salopek, J.J. (1998). Train your brain. *Training and Development,* **52**(10), 26–33.

Sashkin, M., and Walberg, H.J. (1993). *Educational leadership and school culture.* Berkeley, CA: McCutchan Publishing Corporation.

Schraw, G., and Lehman, S. (2001). Situational interest: A review of the literature and directions for future research. *Educational Psychology Review,* **13**, 23–52.

Silverman, D. (2000). *Doing Qualitative Research: A Practical Handbook.* London: SAGE.

Stiles, D.R. (2004). Narcissus revisited: The values of management academics and their role in business school strategies in the UK and Canada. *British Journal of Management,* **15**, 157–175.

Sweeney, J. (1981). Teacher dissatisfaction on the rise: Higher-level needs unfulfilled. *Education,* **102**, 203–207.

Snyder, I., Marginson, S. and Lewis, T. (2007). "An Alignment of the Planets": Mapping the Intersections between Pedagogy, Technology and Management in Australian Universities. *Journal of Higher Education Policy and Management,* **29**(2), 187–202.

Trusty, F.M., and Sergiovanni, T.J. (1966). Perceived need deficiencies of teachers and administrators: A proposal for restructuring teacher roles. *Educational Administration Quarterly,* **2**, 168–180.

Tschannen-Moran, M., and Woolfolk Hoy, A.E. (2001). Teacher efficacy: Capturing an elusive construct. *Teaching and Teacher Education,* **17**, 783–805.

Whitchurch, C. (2006). Who do they think they are? The changing identities of professional administrators and managers in UK higher education. *Journal of Higher Education Policy and Management,* **28**(2), 159–171.

Wright, M.D. (1985). *Relationships among esteem, autonomy, job satisfaction and the intention to quit teaching of downstate Illinois industrial education teachers* (Doctoral dissertation, University of Illinois at Urbana-Champaign, 1985). Dissertation Abstracts International, **46**, 3273A.

不闻不若闻之　闻之不若见之　见之不若知之　知之不若行之
学至于行之而止矣。

Hearing about something is better than not hearing about something. Seeing something is better than hearing about something. Knowing something is better than hearing about something. Actually doing something is better than knowing something. In order to totally understand something, you must work hard to attain that knowledge. This means that you can only understand something by trying it yourself.

Dao De Jing

Chapter 3

Reinforcing Regulation
of Private Institutions

This chapter examines the prevalence of private commercial schools in Singapore, many of which may not have met the regulatory requirements if strict monitoring actions were to be applied to them. The majority of private commercial schools in Singapore are small and have no proper facilities such as libraries, student recreation facilities and computer labs. While over 600 schools have been deregistered since 2009, either voluntarily or involuntarily, following the introduction of the Council for Private Education Act in 2009, over 300 schools are still operating. Of these 300 schools, only less than one-fifth can be considered to have proper facilities. The first part of this paper explores the possible reasons why some private commercial schools are still in operation despite not meeting the recommended regulatory guidelines. It suggests stricter actions could be taken by the Council for Private Education to ensure that private commercial schools contribute to the improvement of the overall education landscape in Singapore and makes recommendations where the Council could increase its vigilance on these schools. It also recommends a framework relating to the monitoring and review of the current audit process of private commercial schools. The second part of the paper explores the failure of private commercial schools to deliver quality education to their students and the reasons students are still choosing the private education route as an option for their studies. Contrary to popular assumptions, private commercial schools in Singapore pose no significant competition to public schools. Teachers at private commercial schools do not receive as much training and development as those in public schools. Profit seems to be the main driver for these commercial schools.

Introduction

The significance of this chapter is that it explores the possible reasons why some private commercial schools are still in operation despite not meeting the recommended regulatory guidelines. It also suggests stricter actions should be taken by the Council for Private Education to ensure that private commercial schools contribute to the improvement of the overall education landscape in Singapore and makes recommendations where the Council could increase its vigilance on these schools. It examines the views of students and teachers of four private commercial schools in areas such as teaching quality, students' attendance, school facilities, students' support and counselling, and number of full-time faculty members.

Despite the failure of some private commercial schools to deliver quality education, students are still choosing the private education route as an option for their studies. Principal characteristics or behaviour have a profound impact on school performance (Yu, 2009). They are the main agents of change for improving schools' performance. Teachers' attitudes and effectiveness depend on the incentives they receive. Lavy (2004) found that incentives led to increased student achievement through changes in teaching methods and teachers being more responsive to students' needs. A large amount of literature has investigated the impact of teachers' salaries on student outcomes, with mixed results (Lavy, 2002; Glewwe, Ilias and Kremer, 2003). Teachers of private commercial schools interviewed felt that their peers at public schools were being rewarded higher than them. They saw higher pay as one of the main motivational factors to work harder. This chapter does not aim to present any direct evidence on the educational benefits of increased pay, though the use of incentive payments raises a presumption that it has a positive motivational effect on teachers' commitment and teaching quality.

Contrary to popular assumptions, private commercial schools in Singapore pose no significant competition to public schools. Teachers at private commercial schools do not receive as much training and development as those in public schools. Profit seemed to be the main driver for these commercial schools. With the strong financial support from the government, private commercial schools could not compete with public schools.

This section also concludes that the Edutrust Certification Scheme is unfairly discriminatory against local students. It should be amended and made compulsory for all Private Educational Institutes (PEIs or private schools) regardless of whether they enrol international or local students. Currently, it is a voluntary scheme applicable to those institutions which enrol international students. The original objective of the scheme was to differentiate PEIs with higher standards in key areas of management and the provision of educational services. The fact that it is applicable to institutions which wanted to enrol international students creates an unfair discriminatory effect on local students. This scheme has discriminated unfairly against local students as its main focus is the well-being of the international students. The scheme should be broadened to cover all private schools registered with the Council for Private Education (CPE) and not selectively to those which enrol international students.

Background of the Private Education Industry

A majority of private commercial schools occupy premises of less than 200 square metres with no proper facilities such as libraries, recreational facilities and computer labs. Many schools cut costs by providing only very basic facilities and compromise on teaching quality by hiring unqualified teaching staff. Many of the teaching staff are either part-timers or are unregistered with the Council for Private Education. While many private commercial schools have been deregistered since the implementation of the CPE Act in 2009, many more schools have mushroomed as business enterprises discover creative ways to overcome the restrictions imposed by the CPE Act. There is, thus, a need for the governing authority to check the exploitation of the loopholes in the Act. It needs to review the existing audit processes of private commercial schools to weed out errant school operators. Only through a comprehensive and effective oversight of private commercial schools can it enforce the CPE Act for public good.

While private schools have mushroomed, there are no clear differences in quality between larger schools and smaller schools as many small schools with no proper facilities are awarded a four-year registration status. This gives the public a very misleading picture, as they may perceive the four-year registration status as an endorsement of quality. The attainment of the four-year EduTrust mark does not guarantee that the quality of education provided by the private commercial schools is of high standard. The management of many of these schools have put in much efforts to "dress-up" the school's environment and various records (admission, attendance, staff training and faculty profile) during the audit period process without implementing real changes to its operations.

In January 2016, the Singapore government announced the formation of a new statutory board, the SkillsFuture Singapore (SSG) which will focus on the implementation of SkillsFuture, coordinating pre-employment training and continuing education and training. The CPE, which currently regulates the private-education sector, will be subsumed under the SSG. This is timely as there are a wide variety of training programmes which do not come under the CPE. As the SSG assumes oversight of the private education sector, it should increase the competencies of CPE's auditors and inspectors to include skills such as understanding company accounts in relation to student fees and staff compensation. These two areas are often exploited by the management of private commercial schools and CPE's auditors and inspectors should recognise the skills gaps in their current job roles.

Many smaller private schools are unable to comply with the regulatory requirement of having an Examination Board and Academic Board. Advisory boards play an important role in assessment and improving curriculum. An improved curriculum ensures that students will receive an education responsive to community needs (Taylor, Marino, Rasor-Greenhalgh and Hudak, 2010). While members of the Examination Board are tasked to ensure the quality of the programs, the assessment process and learning outcomes, many of those listed as members of the Examination and Academic Boards are not actively involved with these processes. The inclusion of their names with their impressive credentials in the school websites should be considered deceptive business practices if they are not actively engaged in developing examination and assessment procedures, moderating examination and assessment marks and handling appeals from students with regards to examination or assessment matters.

The independence of the Academic and Examination Board has often been compromised in private commercial schools as very often the school's management dictates the curriculum, the assessment criteria and examination matters. Advisory Board members offer support to institution administrators and faculty (Conroy, Lefever, and Withiam, 1996). They comprised accomplished experts offering innovative advice and dynamic perspectives (Stautberg and Green, 2007). In some private commercial schools, the principals took the initiative to change the examination marks of students without consulting the other Examination Board members. This conflict of interests of the school principal is evident as he may serve multiple roles as the CEO, principal, member of Academic Board and member of Examination Board.

Another area of concern is the number of qualified full-time lecturers. All private commercial schools face difficulties in recruiting full-time lecturers. The 2014 annual report of the CPE showed that there are 16,079 teachers and that 36% of this figure (5,788) are on full-time basis. This figure requires further investigation as it gives an average of 19 full-time teachers to each school, based on the figure of 312 schools as at end 2014. Many large private commercial schools do not have such a high figure of full-time teachers. They normally engage part-time teachers which may teach in more than one school. The trend is for most institutions to use part-time lecturers to reduce labour costs (Alston, 2010). Part-time teachers have become an important cost-cutting strategy for many schools (Allen-Collinson and Hockey, 1998). The CPE needs to relook at the teachers who have been registered with more than one school and ensure that schools do not just list the names of the teachers in their website to give an impression that they have sufficient qualified teachers. This has negative implications for students as part-time teachers may not be able to commit to teach at a particular school if he has already had a prior commitment with another school. Part-time lecturers face the insecurity of their employment relationship and the dilemma between the need to earn an income and attending to their personal development (Allen-Collinson and Hockey, 1998; Bryson, 1988; Hey, 2001). In such instance, the school may opt for a less-qualified or unqualified teacher as a replacement. This will lead to an inferior class of part-time lecturers which serve as shock absorbers (Entin, 2005). Part-timers are likely to be less prepared for classes and their availability for further consultations is minimal. These factors will affect the learning process of students negatively and lead to the decline of quality education.

Purpose of the Study

The purpose of this section was to ascertain the probable reasons some small private commercial schools are still operating despite not having proper facilities. The study examined the perceptions of students regarding the quality of education in their private commercial schools. It also ascertained the perceptions of teachers regarding the availability of motivating factors in their schools. Finally, it made some recommendations which the governing authorities could adopt to ensure that private commercial schools are contributing to the improvement of quality education in Singapore.

Research Questions

Consequently, the study intends to answer the following research questions:

(1) What are some of the reasons smaller private commercial schools are still operating despite not having proper facilities?
(2) What do students feel about the quality of education in their schools?
(3) What are the motivating factors for teachers?
(4) What recommendations could be made to the governing authorities, specifically the Council for Private Education?

Organisation of the Study

This chapter consists of five sections. The first section includes background information, research objectives and research questions. The second section consists of review of literatures relating to the study and the third section describes the research methodology. Section four covers the presentation of the research findings. The fifth section presents recommendations and conclusions derived from the findings as they relate to the importance of greater supervision of private commercial schools by the relevant authorities.

Review of the Literature

There have been many concerns about the relatively lax regulatory environment which has enabled the establishment of private schools where they are not commercially viable or where there are other issues which should preclude them from setting up (Nicholls, 2004). Financial and regulatory controls are inadequate or have been selectively ignored. Those planning to establish new schools or are running existing schools know the loopholes in the CPE Act and this has enabled them to circumvent existing rules and policies.

Many studies have shown that private schools are superior to public schools, in terms of educational efficiency and cost-effectiveness (Jiminez, Lockheed and Wattanawaha 1988; Kingdon 1994; Govinda and Varghese 1993). However, this may not be the case in Singapore where public schools receive substantial funding from the government.

Mowday, Steers and Porter (1979) concluded that employee commitment to an organisation depends on three factors: (1) strong identification with the organisational goals and values; (2) willingness to "go an extra mile" and (3) a strong desire to remain with the organisation. Shore and Martin (1989) conducted studies to attempt to link organisational commitment with desirable work outcomes such as increased employee satisfaction, improved attendance, improved job performance and a reduction in employee turnover. Similarly, Baruch (1998) concluded that high organisational commitment lead to workforce stability in terms of fewer turnovers and higher attendance. Numerous research studies have been carried out to identify the antecedents of organisational commitment. Hawkins (1998) noted that perceived autonomy, perceived organisational support, and perceived support as the primary predictors of organisational commitment in his studies of school principals.

It is important to note that organisational commitment cannot be expected without reciprocity (Aityan and Gupta, 2012). To gain high levels of commitment from employees, an organisation is expected to show a similar or even higher level of commitments to its employees.

School climate and school culture

School climate characterizes the school at the building and classroom level while school culture is the shared values, attitudes and beliefs that give the school its identity and standard for expected behaviour. Reid, Hopkins and Holy (1987) in their research study listed the characteristics of effective schools as having strong and skilled principals, clearly autonomous management, conducive school climate, clear and consistent school discipline, teacher accountability for student learning and professional development, coordination of curriculum, favourable student–teacher relationship, conducive environment, high expectation of student learning and small school size. Lee and Smith (1993) showed that higher academic achievements are associated with smaller schools, and that being small is a characteristic of private school. The school climate is a significant factor affecting teachers' motivation (Anderson, 1982; Hoy and Miskel, 1996).

Major components which contribute to a school climate include school appearance, faculty relations, students' interactions, leadership, disciplined environment, learning environment, school–community relations. Broadly, we can categorise the school climate into: (a) physical environment, (b) social environment, (c) affective environment and (d) academic environment (Fig. 1).

Research studies have shown that school climate has a significant impact on student's physical and mental health. The school climate affects the self-esteem of students (Hoge, Smith and Hanson, 1990). It is strongly correlated with the emotional and health outcomes of students (Power, Higgins and Kholberg, 1989; Scochet, Dadds, Ham and Montague, 2006; Way, Reddy and Rhodes, 2007). A positive school climate has also been shown to reduce student absenteeism (DeJung and Duckworth, 1986; Purkey and Smith, 1983; Reid, 1982; Rumberger, 1987; Sommer, 1985) and gives lower rates of suspension (Wu, Pink, Crain, and Moles, 1982).

Many private commercial schools in Singapore do not have a strong school culture. They may have a Vision and Mission statement, but that does not adequately reflect the school culture. A school culture that

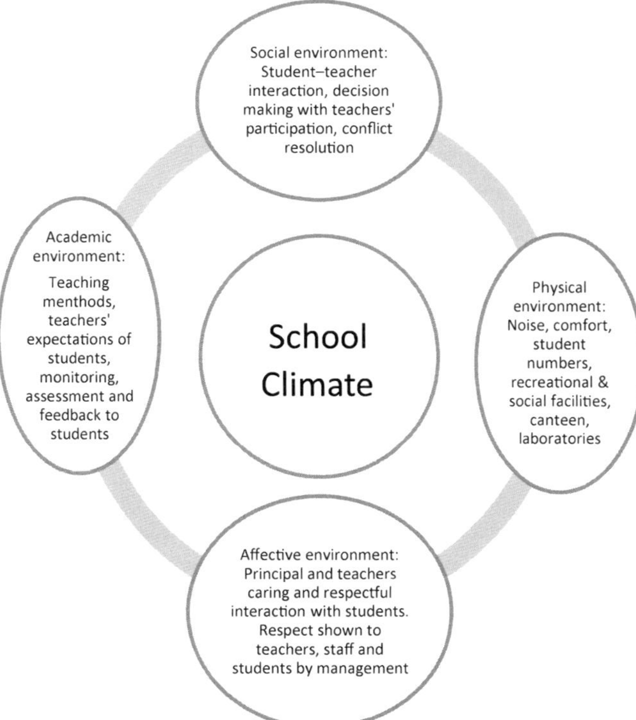

Fig. 1:   School climate.

supports learning will encompass values whereby administrators, teachers, students and parents participate in decision-making. Conversely, a school culture which impedes learning involves making decisions without the participation of teachers and parents. The school culture is influenced by the students and their social class background. Thrupp (1997) reiterated that the social mix of the school affects how it functions. Students who attend the school favour it in a certain way through their own student culture. Deal and Kennedy (1983) stressed that each school has a different reality of mindset of school life. Real improvement in private commercial schools can only come about through the changing mindset of the school administrators. It is not just about changing the school curricula, teaching and learning strategies, assessment structures and entry requirements. It involves placing academic quality as the main objective rather than profit-making as the main objective (Yu, 2009). Sustainable improvement of private commercial schools depends on its ability to reculture. Reculturing is the process of developing new values, beliefs, and norms. It involves transforming mindsets, paradigms, images, beliefs and shared meanings.

School policy

Sanders and Krautman (1995) suggested that entering private schools could reduce the dropout rate of students significantly. Lee and Bryk (1989) and Raudenbush and Bryk (1986) found that student achievement of private Catholic schools was greater than those in public schools. Lee, Smith and Croninger (1997) stated that student achievement was associated with school organisation of curriculum and instruction. Private school students' higher achievement can be attributed to the excellent school organisation. Schools which emphasise student academic achievement showed lower absenteeism (Heyns, 1978).

Teacher friendship for students has a significant correlation with students' academic achievement. Reid, Hopkins and Holy (1987) found that class teacher attitude has an effect on students' academic achievement.

School structure

Chubb and Moe (1990) stressed that political environment affects school organisations. Public schools are more bureaucratic and are accountable to many stakeholders. The structure of the school affects its values and beliefs. Private schools are subject to the forces of competition and they have more freedom to hire and fire teachers. Hirschhorn (1997) recommended the movement of the traditional school structure towards multidirectional communication and away from top–down hierarchical structures. Hoy and Sweetand (2001), and Langer (1992, 1997) emphasised self-reliance and self-worth among teachers by advocating empowerment of teachers. Rousseau (1978) asserted that an organisation with formalised rules and procedures have a strong correlation with absenteeism, the propensity to leave the organisation, physical and psychological stress, and job dissatisfaction. There is a high level of frustration associated with bureaucratic controls (Bonjean and Grimes, 1970)

Teacher motivation

A key determinant of job satisfaction is remuneration. Salary has been the greatest motivational issues for private commercial schools teachers. Teachers' salaries at private commercial schools are relatively lower than their counterparts at public schools. (Table 1). This is due to the strong emphasis by the government to attract good teachers to public schools. Private commercial schools face stiff competition from public institutions to recruit qualified full-time teachers and have to opt for more part-time teachers.

Besides salary, the motivation of teachers is affected by factors such as social economic status, classroom environment, students' behaviour and respect from principals. School leadership and management style can either motivate or lower teacher morale and commitment. Teachers feel highly motivated when they are being consulted about decisions regarding their work. Conversely, unfair administrative and supervisory practices tend to demotivate teachers. Teachers who experience a low level of job satisfaction are more likely to leave (Steel and Ovalle, 1984). Promoting teachers without proper appraisal and evaluation mechanism also tends to demotivate teachers. A high-handed and autocratic principal dealing with teachers tends to lower teacher morale.

Demotivated teachers tend to have a negative impact on student performance. Teachers who are highly motivated will raise the self-esteem of their students (Peck, Fox, and Morston (1977). Students see teachers as their role models. There are significant differences in the scores of students

Table 1:   Salary grade by qualification, SGD/month.

	Private Commercial Schools	Public Schools	Public Higher Learning Institutes
Masters	3,500–4,500	4,500–6,500	5,000–7,000
Doctorate	4,000–5,000	5,500–7,500	6,500–12,000

taught by teachers with high job satisfaction and of those taught by teachers with low job satisfaction (Brumback, 1986). A motivated teacher will generally be satisfied with his job. This motivation will then bring about positive learning attitudes and self-esteem of the students.

School management needs to pay particular attention to the way they deal with teachers. Treating teachers with respect, providing good working environment and developing teacher skills and competencies will motivate teachers to perform better. Sirgy (1986) stressed that when the higher order needs such as esteem and self-actualisation needs are met, teachers will move towards a higher level of development. The more motivated teachers are, the greater commitment they will place in their work. When teachers see that their students are progressing and achieving their targets, they become motivated as their esteem needs have been met. Motivated teachers direct their work towards achieving their goals of teaching (Vroom, 1964; McClelland, 1985; Maehr, 1984).

Studies by Wilby (1989) found that teachers were motivated when they were involved in discussions regarding school policies and when they are valued as professionals. Principal leadership behaviours and organisational structures affect teachers' job satisfaction (Miskel, 1974, 1979; Yu, 2009). Principals' recognition of teachers' contribution and professional development of teachers have a high correlation to teachers' productivity (Holdaway, 1978).

Figure 2 illustrates a cycle whereby principals first motivate teachers, who in turn motivate students. The higher the students' achievement, the more motivated are the teachers. It is, therefore, essential that principals pay attention to the way they interact with teachers.

Methodology

The research study was carried out on four private commercial schools in the Western and Central part of Singapore, using both qualitative and quantitative methods. Two of the schools could be categorised as small with fewer than 100 students while the other two have between 100 to 200 students. The two larger schools are located in the Central part of Singapore while the smaller schools are located in the West. A random sample of 100 students and 12 teachers were interviewed.

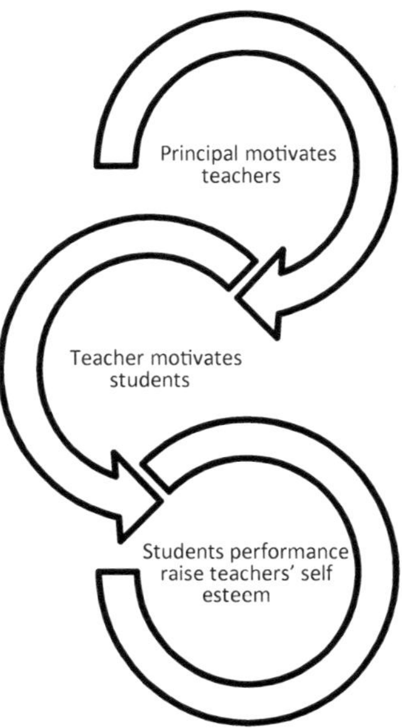

Fig 2:   Motivation cycle.

Two researchers were appointed to be engaged in interviews and collection of other relevant data from the students. The student sample consists of 55 male students and 45 female students. The students were interviewed outside their schools to avoid any pre-prepared answers and also not to alarm the schools' principals. Approximately 20 students were interviewed from each of the small school while 30 students were interviewed from each of the larger school. The students were interviewed regarding curriculum, student support, school facilities, commitment of teachers and classroom size. The data was collected over a four-week period.

A typical 5-point ordinal Likert scale was used by the respondent to rate the degree to which they agree or disagree with the interview statement. The students and teachers were given different sets of questionnaires to measure the attitudes or opinions under investigation.

The students were asked to fill up a survey form which consisted of 20 questions. Survey respondents were asked to give their views on how much they agreed with the statements relating to curriculum, student support, facilities and adherence to school policies. No incentives were provided for the participants and their participation was entirely on a voluntary basis. During the interviews, different prompts and probes were used to encourage participants to talk and in their own way (Drever, 1995). Prompts and probes may include questions like "are you sure?" and "why is that so?" to get the participants to clarify an answer or explain further.

Four teachers from the each of the two larger schools and two teachers from each of the smaller schools were contacted through e-mails to gather their participation in the interview process. A set of questionnaires were sent to the teachers' e-mail. The teachers were asked to give their views on the motivational factors in their jobs. They were interviewed regarding their issues relating to salary, experience, qualifications, training and development, welfare and benefits, students performance, students attendance, and students profile.

Protection of Privacy

To ensure the protection of privacy, all participants were given a consent form to sign prior to the data collection process. The consent form explained the purpose of this study, stressed that participation was voluntary and that participants were free to withdraw from the study if they so wished. To protect the confidentiality of participants and the private commercial schools, numerical codes have been used in reporting the findings.

Results and Discussions

Analysis of students' survey

Table 2 shows the mean and standard deviations of the different variables. The variable "fairness" has the highest mean with 3.13, followed by "school environment" with mean of 3.1 and "receiving quality feedback" with mean of 3.07. The variable "fairness" has a standard deviation of 1.05 which meant that there is a wide dispersion in the sampling distribution of the sample mean. Similar situations exist for the variables "school environment" and "receiving quality feedback" with standard deviations of 1.07 and 0.99, respectively. The large standard deviations reflect a large amount of variations in the sample being studied.

Table 2:   Descriptive statistics.

	N	Minimum	Maximum	Mean	Std. Deviation
Choice	100	1.00	5.00	2.9200	0.87247
Stressed	100	1.00	5.00	2.8400	0.99209
Well-being	100	1.00	5.00	2.9800	0.90988
Opportunity	100	1.00	5.00	2.9100	0.91115
Feedback	100	1.00	5.00	3.0700	0.99752
Money	100	1.00	4.00	2.7400	0.76038
Enthusiastic	100	1.00	5.00	3.0400	0.97359
Qualified	100	1.00	5.00	2.6100	1.00398
Concerned	100	1.00	5.00	3.0300	0.92611
Curriculum	100	1.00	4.00	2.8100	0.77453
Discipline	100	1.00	4.00	2.3600	0.92682
Control	100	1.00	5.00	2.3900	0.88643
Attendance	100	1.00	4.00	2.3500	0.83333
Absenteesim	100	1.00	4.00	2.2400	0.81798
Respect	100	1.00	5.00	2.5200	0.95853
Fairness	100	1.00	5.00	3.1300	1.05078
Facilities	100	1.00	5.00	3.0000	0.88763
Environment	100	1.00	5.00	3.1000	1.07778
Rules	100	1.00	5.00	2.8600	0.87640
Recommendation	100	1.00	5.00	2.9700	0.88140
Valid N (listwise)	100				

Schools should assess how students feel about their school. If a student feels that the school does not care about him, it will impact the student's behaviour in classroom and his motivation in class. Studies have shown that a high-quality school climate may counter the negative effects of self-criticism and low levels of learning abilities.

The variable with the lowest mean is "absenteeism" with mean of 2.24. This essentially indicates that students place very little emphasis on school attendance and do not see attendance as an important factor. "Enforcement of discipline" is another concern, with a mean of 2.36. Students do not see adherence to school discipline as important and have placed very low priority in this factor.

School climate affects the student's perception of belonging and closeness with others at the school (Loukas, 2007). A student who feels connected to the school will be less likely to be absent (deJung and Duckworth, 1986; Purkey and Smith, 1983; Reid, 1982; Rumberger, 1987; Sommer, 1985). Principals should implement programs to improve school climate. These include: (a) upgrading teachers knowledge and skills; (b) ensuring order and safety; (c) enhancing parent-school-community ties; and (d) improving curriculum and instructional guidance.

Table 3 contains a column containing "Corrected Item-Total Correlation" for each of the items. It displays the correlation between a

Table 3:   Item-total statistics.

	Scale Mean if Item Deleted	Scale Variance if Item Deleted	Corrected Item-Total Correlation	Squared Multiple Correlation	Cronbach's Alpha if Item Deleted
Choice	52.9500	98.917	0.845	0.938	0.883
Stressed	53.0300	110.575	0.133	0.248	0.903
Well-being	52.8900	99.392	0.778	0.908	0.885
Opportunity	52.9600	99.029	0.798	0.931	0.884
Feedback	52.8000	100.162	0.660	0.730	0.888
Money	53.1300	103.003	0.697	0.607	0.888
Enthusiastic	52.8300	105.981	0.370	0.423	0.897
Qualified	53.2600	113.245	0.004	0.348	0.907
Concerned	52.8400	105.833	0.401	0.382	0.895
Curriculum	53.0600	104.845	0.561	0.514	0.891
Discipline	53.5100	103.970	0.503	0.677	0.893
Control	53.4800	103.686	0.546	0.843	0.891
Attendance	53.5200	104.131	0.559	0.851	0.891
Absenteesim	53.6300	105.407	0.492	0.804	0.893
Respect	53.3500	108.977	0.222	0.577	0.901
Fairness	52.7400	104.255	0.418	0.553	0.895
Facilities	52.8700	102.498	0.615	0.616	0.889
Environment	52.7700	101.936	0.516	0.550	0.892
Rules	53.0100	99.364	0.813	0.958	0.884
Recommend	52.9000	99.768	0.783	0.911	0.885

given variable and the sum of the other variables. For example, the correlation between "Choice" and the sum of the other variables is 0.845. What this means is that there is a strong positive correlation between "Choice" and all other variables. This indicates that the students' assessment of whether a school is their choice school is influenced by many other factors such as school environment, well-being, attendance, and so on.

We also investigated the dimensionality of the scale by using the Principal Component Analysis. Internal consistency is concerned with the interrelatedness of the test items while homogeneity measures the degree of unidimensionality. The concept of reliability assumes that unidimensionality exists in a sample of test items.

From Table 4, we are able to analyse the Eigen Values of the various items. Eigen Values tell us how much of the variances in the items are captured by the factors. We see that the Eigen Value for the first factor accounted for 40.9% of the total variance, the second factor 18.4%, the third 7.8% and fourth 5.5%. All the other remaining factors are not significant.

The Extracted Sum of Square Loadings columns showed four rows which correspond to the number of factors retained. The values in this panel are based on the common variance and are smaller than the total variance.

Table 4:   Total variance explained.

	Initial Eigenvalues			Extraction Sums of Squared Loadings		
Component	Total	% of Variance	Cumulative %	Total	% of Variance	Cumulative %
1	8.185	40.923	40.923	8.185	40.923	40.923
2	3.686	18.429	59.352	3.686	18.429	59.352
3	1.572	7.859	67.211	1.572	7.859	67.211
4	1.094	5.471	72.682	1.094	5.471	72.682
5	0.925	4.625	77.308			
6	0.676	3.378	80.686			
7	0.644	3.218	83.904			

Extraction method: Principal component analysis.

Table 5:   Reliability statistics.

Cronbach's Alpha	Cronbach's Alpha Based on Standardised Items	N of Items
0.897	0.903	20

The Cronbach's Alpha is chosen as a measure of internal consistency or reliability. The acceptable values of alpha ranges from 0.70 to 0.95 (Devellis, 2003; Nunnally and Bernstein, 1994). Values of between 0.71 and 0.80 represent a good reliability, and between 0.81 and 0.95 is considered to be very good reliability (Zikmund *et al.*, 2010; Sekaran and Bougie, 2010). Table 5 shows a Cronbach's Alpha of 0.897 which indicates a high level of internal consistency for our scale. This means that respondents who select high scores for one item also select high scores for the others. Likewise, those who select low scores for one item will also select low scores for the other items.

The column on "Cronbach's Alpha if Deleted" indicates that removal of a variable will improve the overall Cronbach Alpha. For example, the removal of Question 2 which relates to the variable "stress" faced by students would lead to small improvement in Cronbach's Alpha and we could see that the "Corrected Item-Total Correlation" was a low 0.133 for this item. Similarily, the removal of the variable "respect" will improve the Cronbach Alpha marginally to 0.901. However, as the "Corrected Item-Total Correlation" was much higher at 0.222, we may consider retaining this item in the questionnaire.

Analysis of teachers' survey

Table 6 shows the means and standard deviations of the different variables. The variables "salary", "training", "recognition", and "teaching requirements" all have means above 4. This meant that many teachers are dissatisfied with their current schools. The low standard deviations of below 1 indicate that all their views are quite similar in the sample being studied.

Principals of private commercial schools must develop the necessary skills to manage a school. While some skills may be developed through formal principalship training, others are learned while on the job.

Table 6:   Descriptive statistics.

	N	Minimum	Maximum	Mean	Std. Deviation
Salary	15	3.00	5.00	4.4000	0.63246
Underpaid	15	2.00	5.00	4.0667	0.88372
Incentive	15	1.00	3.00	1.8667	0.83381
Leadership	15	3.00	5.00	3.6667	0.81650
Principal value	15	2.00	5.00	3.2667	0.96115
Training	15	3.00	5.00	4.2667	0.79881
Recognition	15	4.00	5.00	4.1333	0.35187
Fairness	15	3.00	5.00	3.8667	0.63994
Satisfaction	15	3.00	5.00	3.6667	0.81650
Teaching	15	3.00	5.00	4.0667	0.79881
Teaching resource	15	2.00	4.00	2.8667	0.74322
Student committment	15	2.00	5.00	3.4667	1.06010
Student quality	15	1.00	5.00	3.5333	1.30201
Low entry	15	1.00	3.00	1.8667	0.74322
Attendance	15	1.00	4.00	2.4667	0.74322
High marks	15	1.00	5.00	2.2667	1.22280
Staff well–being	15	1.00	3.00	2.3333	0.72375
Student well–being	15	1.00	4.00	2.4667	0.99043
Branding	15	2.00	5.00	3.6667	1.11270
Workplace	15	2.00	5.00	3.0667	0.79881
Valid N (listwise)	15				

Principals have to cultivate relationships with their staff and their attempts to be successful within the school environment is dependent on their leadership styles (Scribner, Hage and Warne, 2002).

Improvement of relationships with teachers must be a core strategy for change. How principals interaction with teachers will determine the educational setting of the school. Deal and Peterson (1998) define school culture as "the underground streams of norms, values, beliefs, traditions and rituals that have built up over time as people work together, solve problems and confront challenges".

Principals need to have better communication with teachers and be aware of the various factors which motivate them. From our survey, teachers agree that giving incentives will be a way of motivating them. Pay-for-performance or merit pay is a powerful motivational tool when used effectively. High performers prefer performance-based pay systems more than low performers. Incentive pay for teachers can be in various forms such as career ladder pay, merit pay, and pay for performance (Hatry and Greiner, 1994).

A major concern arises in the entry requirements of students. Teachers felt that the schools have not adhered to the entry requirements and have accepted students without the proper qualifications. Students who do not meet the entry requirements are more likely to perform poorly in school and this demotivates teachers. While profit motive may undermine private commercial schools strict adherence to entry requirements, principals have often compromised the professionalism of teachers by admitting unqualified students. This may include students who have not attained the proper English language proficiency or who have not meet the basic academic qualifications for entry into a program.

Training and development is another area which have not received high priority in private commercial schools as principals are not willing to invest in upgrading the skills of lecturers and staff for fear that they may leave after gaining the additional skills and knowledge. Training and development promote significant and worthwhile change in teachers' practice and principals need to be supportive of this if they are determined to bring about improvement in the school. Teachers need to develop not only the factual knowledge but also the procedural knowledge of when, how and under what conditions to apply their new skills.

Table 7 contains a column containing "Corrected Item-Total Correlation" for each of the item. It displays the correlation between a given variable and the sum of the other variables. For example, the correlation between "Satisfaction" and the sum of the other variables is 0.545. What this means is that there is a strong positive correlation between "Satisfaction" and all other variables. This indicates that the teacher satisfaction is being influenced by many other factors such as salary incentive, principal value and so on.

Teacher job satisfaction is influenced by factors such as participation in school decision-making, influence over school policy, control in the

Table 7:   Corrected Item-Total Correlation.

	Scale Mean if Item Deleted	Scale Variance if Item Deleted	Corrected Item-Total Correlation	Cronbach's Alpha if Item Deleted
Salary	60.8667	46.838	0.046	0.720
Underpaid	61.2000	45.600	0.105	0.720
Incentive	63.4000	45.543	0.124	0.717
Leadership	61.6000	47.400	−0.038	0.730
Principal value	62.0000	41.857	0.391	0.693
Training	61.0000	43.000	0.382	0.696
Recognition	61.1333	47.838	−0.067	0.721
Fairness	61.4000	43.686	0.419	0.696
Satisfaction	61.6000	41.257	0.545	0.681
Teaching	61.2000	42.171	0.465	0.689
Teaching resource	62.4000	43.114	0.407	0.695
Students committment	61.8000	40.314	0.461	0.685
Student quality	61.7333	40.638	0.320	0.702
Low entry	63.4000	43.971	0.316	0.702
Attendance	62.8000	42.171	0.509	0.687
Highmarks	63.0000	40.000	0.397	0.691
Staff well–being	62.9333	44.924	0.226	0.708
Student well–being	62.8000	40.886	0.456	0.686
Branding	61.6000	46.686	−0.019	0.738
Workplace	62.2000	44.886	0.198	0.711

classroom and recognition of contribution. Blasé and Balse (1994) showed that principals using shared governance strategies and participatory management were able to motivate teachers and give them a sense of ownership and empowerment. Principals need to know how best to motivate teachers to bring about improved performance of teachers, which in turn bring about improved performance of students.

The column on "Cronbach's Alpha if Deleted" indicates that removal of a variable will improve the overall Cronbach Alpha. For example, the removal of Question 19 which relates to the variable "branding" would lead to small improvement in Cronbach's Alpha.

Table 8:   Total variance explained.

Component	Initial Eigenvalues			Extraction Sums of Squared Loadings		
	Total	% of Variance	Cumulative %	Total	% of Variance	Cumulative %
1	4.188	20.941	20.941	4.188	20.941	20.941
2	3.350	16.749	37.691	3.350	16.749	37.691
3	2.322	11.608	49.298	2.322	11.608	49.298
4	2.166	10.830	60.128	2.166	10.830	60.128
5	1.805	9.027	69.155	1.805	9.027	69.155
6	1.785	8.923	78.078	1.785	8.923	78.078
7	1.128	5.642	83.720	1.128	5.642	83.720
8	1.035	5.175	88.895	1.035	5.175	88.895
9	0.760	3.802	92.697	—	—	—

Extraction method: Principal component analysis.

Table 8 shows the Eigenvalues of the various items. Eigenvalues tell us how much of the variances in the items are captured by the factors. We see that the Eigenvalue for the first factor accounted for 20.9% of the total variance, the second factor 16.7%, the third 11.6% and fourth 10.8%. A total of eight factors have been chosen.

The Extracted Sum of Square Loadings columns showed eight rows which correspond to the number of factors retained. The values in this panel are based on the common variance and are smaller than the total variance.

Johnson (1986) suggested three theories of motivation and productivity: Expectancy theory which describes that individuals are more likely to work if there is an anticipated reward that they value; Equity theory which states that individuals are dissatisfied if they are not justly compensated for their efforts and accomplishments; and Job enrichment theory which indicates that workers are more productive when their work is challenging and varied.

Table 9 shows a Cronbach's Alpha of 0.715 which indicates a high level of internal consistency for our scale. This means that respondents who select high scores for one item also select high scores for the others. Likewise, those who select low scores for one item will also select low scores for the other items.

Table 9: Reliability statistics.

Cronbach's Alpha	Cronbach's Alpha Based on Standardized Items	N of Items
0.715	0.708	20

Recommended New Compliance Audit Framework

This new audit framework addresses the current shortcomings of the current audit process. The shortcomings have given the opportunity to private commercial schools operators to circumvent the various requirements of the Private Education Regulations of the CPE Act. The areas which require special focus include the following:

(1) Enrolment Verification
(2) Attendance
(3) Entry Requirements
(4) Training & Learning
(5) Program Approval
(6) Registration of faculty (Full Time and Part Time)
(7) Compliance with Accounting Policies

The non-adherence to school procedures by principals is mainly due to the pressures of increasing students numbers. They may compromise academic quality and be pressured by students to pass or raise the students' exam marks (Fig. 3).

A robust compliance program is essential to ensure that private commercial schools comply with their obligations under the relevant legislation (CPE Act) and that instances of non-compliance are addressed by enforcement or other actions.

The new framework promotes effective monitoring and review of the current processes by requiring CPE auditors and inspectors to look at loopholes which are exploited by private education providers. Achieving audit quality requires careful audit and quality control procedures. Such a disciplined and structured approach would encompass careful planning of the audit process as well as impromptu and unannounced visits to private commercial schools. It is imperative that when auditors and inspectors perform the audit, they understand the particular school's environment at normal times and not just during the audit period where many insincere

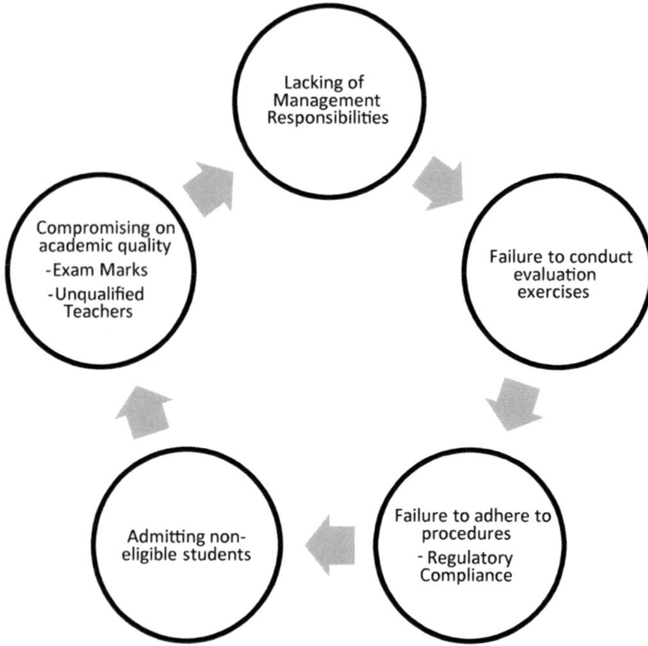

Fig. 3: Common non-compliance areas.

efforts have been put in by the school administrators to project an image of efficiency and compliance.

The new audit framework takes into account the four elements of education institutions (Dimmock, 2007). The first element of Organisational Structure involves how human and physical resources are established and deployed. The second element of Leadership, Management and Decision-Making Processes deals with leadership styles and performance appraisals. The third element of Curriculum looks at the objectives, breadth and depth, and relevance of the curriculum offered. The last element of Teaching and Learning examines the delivery of courses, teacher-student relationship and learning outcomes.

This section recommends the establishment of a new framework for compliance audit incorporating the various variables in our question-naires. With the new framework, auditors and inspectors of private commercial schools could have a tool to improve on the existing audit processes of private commercial schools.

Recommendations, Limitations, and Conclusion

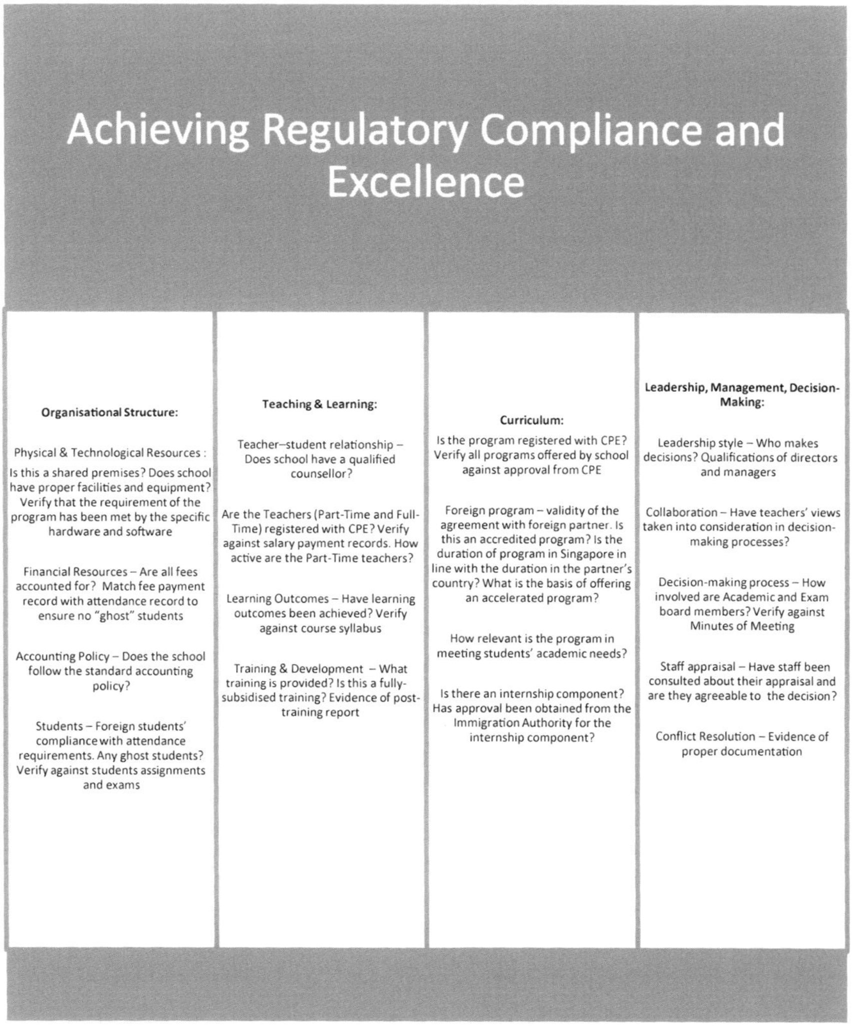

Fig. 4: Recommendation for a new compliance audit framework.

Recommendations of Items to be Included in Compliance Audit Checklist

Figure 4 shows the items which are to be included in the audit checklist.

Enrolment verification

Objective: To ensure that all students enrolled in the school are accounted for.

— Identify the presence of phantom (ghost) students. Match students record with fee payment record.
— Match attendance record with transcripts.
— Match foreign student record with attendance record.
— Verify that students meet the entry requirements. Match student admission record with transcripts to ensure that all students sit for the required tests or exams.

Revenue/reimbursement

Objective: To ensure that financial records reflect all the funds collected from students and refunded to students.

— Student fees — Verify that all fees are accounted for and match them with students' attendance record.
— Highlight any contribution in kind not accounted for.
— Verify the use of standard accounting policies.

Training and learning

— Staff training and development provided by external parties or in-house training.
— Match with invoices and payment record.
— Evidence of post-training report.

Faculty members

To ensure that the faculty members listed in the website are actually involved in teaching at the school

— Full-time faculty members — Verify against salary record
— Part-time — match against pay slip. Determine the level of involvement of part-time teachers over a certain period
— Part-time faculty — Are they registered with the Council for Private Education?

Academic and examination board members

— To ensure that the academic and examination board members are contributing to the assessment and examination processes in the school. Verify against documentary evidence of level of activity and regularity of involvement. Evidence of minutes of meeting

Programs

— Are foreign programs offered accredited by reputable organisations?
— Are all programs offered registered with the Council for Private Education?
— Lecture notes in line with the course curriculum and teaching plan
— Verify achievement of learning outcomes against course syllabuses
— Are the programs offered on an accelerated basis? If so, what is the reason for the shortened duration as compared to the duration at partner's institution? Evidence of proper course matching by partner institution.

Award of diploma

— Match against transcripts. Have students fulfilled the graduation requirements?

Physical facilities/equipment

— Are there sufficient facilities and equipment to conduct the class?

Limitations of Study

The main limitation of the study is the small sample size. The study focused only on private commercial schools and did not cover other private schools. In the future, further studies could be done to analyse the contribution of all private schools in Singapore. These could include private international schools, arts schools, tutorial schools and enrichment schools.

The other difficulty is getting the cooperation of the principals of the private schools as they were unwilling to participate in the survey. The small sample size of both the students and teachers could reduce the statistical accuracy and reliability in analysis. Further research needs to be conducted on how principals of private commercial schools motivate their teachers and non-academic staff.

The differences between responses from male and female students and male and female teachers were not investigated. Male and females may have different preferences and interpretations of factors which may be of importance to them. It would be worthwhile to conduct further studies in this subject area.

Private commercial schools have the choice to not advocate public values and national interests. They have the right to turn away students of different ethnicity and religious backgrounds. There is no need to promote social values as they do not rely on government funding. There is nothing much the authorities could do if they refuse to conform to community values such as inclusiveness and tolerance which the Singapore government is promoting. It is really up to the management of each private school to determine whether it would like to engage in discriminatory practices. The contribution of private commercial schools to the education landscape in Singapore could be a subject of further studies.

Conclusion

From the analysis of the questionnaire to students, we find that some of the reasons students choose private schools include the low entry requirements, the lax attendance policy, the low discipline control and the possibility of pressuring the principal for higher examination marks. This is particularly worrying as such a school environment will have negative implications for both students and teachers. Students who have not met the entry requirements may not have a similar level of knowledge as their other classmates. This may slow down the learning process of the whole class. In addition, teachers will be demotivated to teach those students who should not have been admitted into a program in the first place.

Principals must become more sensitive and aware of their teachers' needs. They have to learn the skills to motivate teachers and to keep teachers' enthusiasm and interest high. Motivated teachers are school assets. The more motivated the teachers, the greater their work commitment. Providing a good working environment and giving teachers more resources are not quite enough as teachers strive towards a higher stage of personal development.

Failure to implement a stringent attendance policy will only encourage "ghost" students to enrol in private commercial schools. Many of these students are working illegally without the approval of the Immigration Department or the Ministry of Manpower. Schools tried to circumvent the 90% attendance policy set by the Immigration Department by declaring false attendance records to the authorities. Students working illegally are a cause of social problems and many private commercial schools are contributing to this problem as profit-making is their main objective.

Principals of private commercial schools are more likely to give in to the pressure from students to increase their exam grades. They may make the decision alone without consultation with the other Examination Board members. As most principals of private commercial schools are also members of the Academic and Examination Boards, there is normally no higher management level person to oversee his actions.

Feedback from students showed that they were generally quite indifferent about the quality of education in their schools. This may be due to their lower expectations of the schools in terms of quality education and facilities. They felt that while the teachers have the qualifications to teach them in class, they are less concerned about the learning outcomes of students. This may be due to a number of demotivating factors of teachers which include the quality of students in class, the attendance of the students, the lack of interaction with students, the salary of the teachers, and the relationship with the principals.

Most teachers at private commercial schools were not satisfied with their job. The reasons include the perception that they are being paid lower than the peers at public schools and public universities. They felt little recognition for their contribution and that the quality of students and their poor attendance were some of the major issues that have not been addressed by the principals.

Private schools, however, remain competitive in Singapore. They cater to students who may not have achieved the basic entry requirements into a program. A large proportion of their students are from overseas and also working adults who may not fit into the rigorous schedule of public schools. The Council for Private Education needs to relook at the ways it monitors private commercial schools for compliance related issues.

The recommended new compliance audit framework serves as a tool to assist CPE auditors and inspectors to conduct a more thorough and diligent assessment of private schools. They have to pay particular attention to the physical facilities, attendance records, entry requirements, and faculty members. Many small private commercial schools operate from premises which have an area of no more than 200 square metres. While many of these schools are owned by entrepreneurs, the authorities have a duty to ensure that there is proper compliance with the regulations and that enforcement actions need to be stepped up to deter errant school owners.

The Edutrust Certification Scheme is unfairly discriminatory against local students. It should be amended and made compulsory for all private schools regardless of whether they enrol international or local students. The original aim of the Edutrust Scheme was to differentiate high-quality schools from low-quality private schools and is only applicable to those private schools which recruit international students. Local students deserve the same protection as international students, regardless of whether they study in an Edutrust certified school or not. Further shake-up is inevitable to weed out low-quality schools. Only then, can the authorities claim that Singapore has a high standard of private education which caters to both local and international students.

References

Aityan, S.K., and Gupta, T.K.P. (2012). Challenges of employee loyalty in corporate America. *Business and Economic Journal*, **55**, 1–13.

Allen-Collinson, J., and Hockey, J. (1998). Capturing Contracts: Informal activity among contract researchers. *British Journal of Sociology of Education*, **19**(4), 497–515.

Alston, L.A. (2010). *Career Management Strategies of Part Time Lecturers in Humanities.* University of Pretoria, Faculty of Education.

Anderson, C. (1982). The search for school climate: a review of the research. *Review of Educational Research*, **52**, 368–420.

Baruch, Y. (1998). The rise and fall of Organizational Commitment, *Human Systems Management*, **17**(2), 135–143.

Blase, J., and Blasé, J. (1994). *Empowering Teachers: What Successful Principals Do.* Thousand Oaks, CA: Corwin Press, Inc.

Blase, J., and Blase, J. (1999). Principals' instructional leadership and teacher development: Teacher perspectives. *Educational Administration Quarterly*, **35**(3), 349–378.

Brumback, C.J. (1986). *The Relationship Between Teacher Job Satisfaction & Student Academic Performance.* Unpublished Doctoral Thesis, Georgia State University.

Bonjean, C.M., and Grimes, M.D. (1970). Bureaucracy and Alienation: A Dimensional Approach. *Social Forces*, **48**(3), 365–373.

Bryson, C. (1998). *More is less: Contract Research in UK higher education institutions.* EASST Conference. Lisbon.

Chubb, J., and Moe, T. (1992). *Politics, Markets and America's Schools.* Washington, D.C. The Brookings Institution.

Conroy, P.A., Lefever, M.M., and Withiam, G. (1996). The value of college advisory boards. *Cornell Hotel and Restaurant Administration Quarterly*, **37**(4), 85–89.

Deal, T.E., and Kennedy, A. (1983). Culture and school performance, *Educational Leadership*, **40**(5), 140–141.

Deal, T.E., and Peterson, K.D. (1998). How Leaders Influence the Culture of Schools. *Educational Leadership*, **56**(1), 28–30.

deJung, J., and Duckworth, K. (1986). *High school teachers and their students' attendance: Final report.* Eugene, OR: University of Oregon Center for Education Policy and Management, College of Education. (ERIC Document Reproduction Service No. ED266557).

DeVellis, R. (2003). *Scale development theory and applications: theory and application.* Thousand Oaks, CA: SAGE.

Drever, E. (1995). *Using Semi-structured Interviews in Small-scale Research: A Teacher's Guide.* Edinburgh: SCRE.

Entin, J. (2005). Contigent Teaching, Corporate Universities and the Academic labour Movement. *Radical Teacher*, **73**, 26–34.

Govinda, R., and Varghese, N.V. (1993): *Quality of Primary Schooling in India: A Case Study of Madhya Pradesh, India.* Paris: UNESCO International Institute for Educational Planning.

Hatry, H.P., Greiner, J.M., and Ashford, B.G. (1994). *Issues and Case Studies in Teacher Incentive Plans* (2nd edn.). Washington, D.C.: The Urban Institute Press.

Hawkins, W.D. (1998). *Predictors of affective organizational commitment among high school principles* (Unpublished doctoral dissertation). Virginia Polytechnic Institute and State University, Virginia.

Hey, V. (2001). The Construction of Academic Time: Subcontracting academic labour in research. *Journal of Education Policy*, **16**(1), 67–84.

Heyns, B. (1978). Summer Learning and the Effects of Schooling. San Diego, CA: Academic Press.

Hills, F.S., Manigan, R.M., and Dow, S.K. (1987). Tracking the theory of merit pay, *Personnel Administrator*, **32**, 50–57.

Hirschhorn, L. (1997). *Reworking authority: Leading and following in a post-modern organization.* Cambridge, MA: The MIT Press.

Hoge, D.R., Smit, E.K., and Hanson, S.L. (1990). School experiences predicting changes in self-esteem of sixth and seventh-grade students. *Journal of Educational Psychology*, **82**, 117–127.

Holdaway, E.A. (1978). *Satisfaction Of Teachers In Alberta With Their Work And Working Conditions.* Edmonton: The University of Alberta.

Hoy, W.K., and Sweetland, S.R. (2001). Designing better schools: The meaning and measure of enabling school structures. *Educational Administration Quarterly*, **37**, 296–321.

Hoy, W.K., and Miskel, C.G. (1996). *Educational Administration: Theory, Research, and Practice* (5th edn.). New York: McGraw-Hill, Inc.

Jimenez, E., Lockheed, M., and Wattanawaha, N. (1988). *The relative efficiency of private and public schools: the case of Thailand,* The World Bank Economic Review **2**(2).

Johnson, S.M. (1986). Incentives for Teachers: What Motivates, What Matters. *Educational Administration Quarterly*, **22**(3), 54–79. doi:10.1177/0013161X86022003003.

Kingdon, Geeta G. (1994). *An Economic Evaluation of School Management-types in India: A Case Study of Uttar Pradesh,* Unpublished D.Phil. thesis, Economics Department, Oxford University.

Langer, E. (1992). *Mindfulness.* Reading, MA: Addison-Wesley.

Langer, E. (1997). *The power of mindful learning.* Reading, MA: Addison-Wesley.

Lavy, V. (2002). Evaluating the Effect of Teachers' Group Performance Incentives on Pupil Achievement. *Journal of Political Economy*, **110**(6), 1286–1317.

Lavy, V. (2004). *Performance Pay and Teachers' Effort, Productivity, and Grading Ethics.* NBER Working Paper w10622, National Bureau of Economic Research, Cambridge, MA.

Lee, V.E., and Bryk, A.S. (1989). A multilevel model of the social distribution of achievement. *Sociology of Education*, **62**, 172–192.

Lee, V., and Smith, J. (1993). Effects of school restructuring on the achievement and engagement of middle-grades students. *Sociology of Education*, **66**(3), 164–187.

Loukas, A (2007). What is School Climate? *Leadership Compass*, **5**(1).

Maehr, M.L., (1984). *Meaning and Motivation: Toward a Theory of Personal Investment.* In: Ames, R.E. and Ames, C. (Eds.). Research On Motivation In Education. New York: Academic Press, Inc.

McClelland, D.C. (1985). *Human Motivation.* Illinois: Scott, Foresman & Co.

Miskel, C. (1974). Intrinsic, Extrinsic And Risk Propensity Factors In The Work Attitudes Of Teachers, Educational Administrators And Business Managers. *Journal of Applied Psychology*, **59**, 339–343.

Mowday, R.T., Steers, R.M., and Porter, L.W. (1979). The measurement of organizational commitment. *Journal of Vocational Behavior*, **14**, 224–247.

Nicholls, J. (2004). *Commonwealth Funding Programs For Private Schools 1996–2004: A favourable climate for expansion and growth,* Paper prepared for the Australian Education Union, http://www.aeufederal.org.au/Debates/jnicholsfund2004.pdf (30 April 2004).

Nunnally, J., and Bernstein, L. (1994). *Psychometric theory.* New York: McGraw-Hill Higher (INC).

Peck, R.F., Fox, R.B., and Morston, P.T. (1977). *Teacher Effects on Students' Achievement and Self-Esteem.* Washington, DC: National Institute of Education.

Power, C., Higgins, A., and Kohlberg, L. (1989). *Lawrence Kohlberg's approach to moral education.* New York: Longman.

Purkey, S., and Smith, M. (1983). Effective schools: a review. *The Elementary School Journal*, **83**(4), 427–452.

Raudenbush, S., and Bryk, S. (1986). A Hierarchical Model for Studying School Effects. *Sociology of Education*, **59**(1), 1–17.

Reid, K., Hopkins, D., and Holly, P. (1987). *Towards the effective school: The problems and some solutions.* Oxford: Basic Blackwell.

Reid, K. (1982). Retrospection and persistent school absenteeism. *Educational Research*, **25**, 110–115.

Richardson, V. (1990). Significant and worthwhile change in teaching practice. *Educational Researcher*, **19**(7), 10–18.

Rousseau, D. (1978). Characteristics of department, positions, and individuals: Contexts for attitude and behavior. *Administrative Science Quarterly*, 23, 521–540.

Rumberger, R. (1987). High school dropouts: A review of issues and evidence. *Review of Education Research*, **57**, 1–29.

Richardson, V. (1990). Significant and worthwhile change in teaching practice. *Educational Researcher*, **19**(7), 10–18.

Sander, W., and Krautman, A. (1995). Catholic schools, dropout rates and attainment. *Economic Inquiry*, **33**(2), 217–233.

Scribner, J.P., Hager, D.R., and Warne, T.R. (2002). The paradox of professional community: Tales from two high schools. *Educational Administration Quarterly*, **38**, 45–76.

Sekaran, U., and Bougie, R. (2009). *Research methods for business.* (5th edn.). British: John Wiley and Sons.

Shochet, I.M., Dadds, M.R., Ham, D., and Montague, R. (2006). School connectedness is an underemphasized parameter in adolescent mental health: Results of a community prediction study. *Journal of Clinical Child & Adolescent Psychology*, **35**, 170–179.

Shore, L.M., and Martin, H.J. (1989). Job satisfaction and organizational commitment in relation to work performance and turnover intentions. *Human Relations*, **42**, 625–638.

Sirgy, M.J. (1986). A Quality-of-Life Theory Derived from Maslow's Developmental Perspective. *American Journal of Economics and Sociology*, **45**(3), 328–342.

Sommer, B. (1985). What's different about truants? A comparison study of eighth graders. *Journal of Youth and adolescence*, **14**, 411–422.

Stautberg, S., and Green, N. (2007). *How an advisory board drives innovation. Boards and Directors,* 52–54. Retrieved from http://www.partner.com.cm/files/Design_Advisory_Board_022607.pdf.

Steel, R.P., and Ovali, N.K. (1984). A review and meta-analysis of the research on the relationship between intention and employee turnover. *Journal of Applied Psychology*, **69**, 673–686.

Taylor, E., Marino, D., Rasor-Greenhalgh, S., and Hudak, S. (2010). Navigating practice and academic change in collaborative partnership with a community advisory board. *Journal of Allied Health*, **39**(3), 103–110.

Thrupp, M. (1997). *The school mix effect; how the social class composition of school intakes shapes school processes and student achievement.* Paper presented to the Annual Meeting of the American Educational Research Association, Chicago.

Vroom, V.H. (1964). *Work Motivation.* New York: Wiley.

Way, N., Reddy, R., and Rhodes, J. (2007). Students' Perceptions of School Climate during Middle School Years: Associations with Trajectories of Psychological and Behavioural Adjustment. *American Journal of Community Psychology*, **40**, 194–213. http://dx.doi.org/10.1007/s10464-007-9143-y.

Wilby, P. (1989). *The Secret Of Successful Schools.* Reproduced in The Straits Times. May 28, 1989:4.

Wu, S., Pink, W., Crain, R., and Moles, O. (1982). Student suspension: A critical reappraisal. *The Urban Review*, **14**(4), 245–303.

Yu, S.O. (2009). Principal Leadership for Private Schools Improvement: The Singapore Perspective. *The Journal of International Social Research*, **2**(6), Winter 2009.

Zikmund, W.G., Babin, B.J., Carr, J.C., and Griffin, M. (2010). *Business research methods.* 8th edn. Canada: South Western.

Appendix 1

Students Survey:

 (1) I feel that I have found the school of my choice
 (2) I feel stressed in class
 (3) I feel that the school is not concerned with our well-being
 (4) I receive sufficient opportunities to demonstrate proficiency on learning
 (5) I receive quality feedback from teachers on my progress in school
 (6) I feel that the school is only concerned with making money
 (7) Most of my teachers are enthusiastic about their teaching
 (8) Most of my teachers are qualified to teach the subjects allocated
 (9) Most of my teachers are concerned about whether I learn in class
(10) Most of the curriculum are planned well
(11) I feel that the discipline in the school is lax
(12) Teachers have little or no control of students in class
(13) I feel that the school does not follow strict attendance policies
(14) Many students skipped class
(15) I feel that the principal does not respect students
(16) The principal deals with problems and conflicts in a fair manner
(17) I feel that the school's facilities are adequate
(18) I feel that the classroom environment is quite comfortable
(19) I feel that school rules are not enforced in any fair way
(20) I will recommend the school to my friends

Appendix 2

SAMPLE SURVEY QUESTIONS FOR STUDENTS

Q1) Do you agree that this is the school of your choice?

☐	☐	☐	☐	☐
Strongly agree	Agree	Neutral	Disagree	Strongly Disagree

Q2) Do you agree that it is stressful in school?

☐	☐	☐	☐	☐
Strongly agree	Agree	Neutral	Disagree	Strongly Disagree

Q3) Do you agree that the school shows concern in your well-being?

☐	☐	☐	☐	☐
Strongly agree	Agree	Neutral	Disagree	Strongly Disagree

工欲善其事, 必先利其器

If a person wants to do a job well, he needs to sharpen his tools first. In other words, you need to prepare to do a job well.

Dao De Jing

Chapter 4

Reculturing Private Universities

This chapter explores the key issues and challenges facing private university leaders today. Universities are reculturing their operational processes, academic content and interactions with stakeholders. Many challenges centre around the need for university leaders to reculture the institutions and the redesigning of the teaching profession. It recommends a framework for university leaders to deal with the challenges they face. Only through reculturing, will private universities be able to maintain sustainability of its workforce and student population. The article has both theoretical and practical significance for private university leaders to follow.

Introduction

This chapter explores the conundrum of private university leadership today. It commences with a review of literature relating to the reculturing of educational institutions and look at the challenges of developing a professional learning community (PLC). The second section proposes a framework of sustainability to share with university leaders. The final section provides some implications of this study for the private higher education sector.

A study by Yu (2012) found that there are four issues and challenges facing university leaders today. These are: (1) ensuring academic freedom; (2) maintaining staff motivation; (3) maintaining academic quality and (4) providing effective leadership. Private university leaders may focus on competing paradigms such as "student as scholars" versus "students as consumers". Snyder *et al.* (2007) and Giroux (2005) noted the interactive forces of mass education and of sound pedagogical principles in university education. The competitive pressure to recruit more students may prompt universities to lower the entry requirements of students, which in turn has negative implications on teacher motivation.

University leaders have different views on delivering education based on sound principles of pedagogy and the need to create efficiencies of mass education (Coaldrake and Stedman, 1999; Meek and Wood, 1997; Pratt and Poole, 1999; Ramsden, 1998). Universities have opted for either larger classes or reduced contact time, or a combination of both due to resource reduction (Longden, 2006).

In today's competitive environment, leaders need to have the courage to take action when the future remains unclear (Barnett, 2004) and Hanna (2003). In the process of developing the university as a learning organisation, the leader has to establish new relationships with all the stakeholders concerned. This chapter examines the notion of leadership as being enabling and capacity building. It discusses through a process of reculturing the university as learning organisations, new capacities are being developed (Lingard, Hayes, Mills and Christies, 2003; Hargreaves, 2003).

Universities have to maintain a sustainable workforce to remain competitive. Workforce sustainability is about attracting and retaining the right people with the right skills and competencies, to meet the current and future needs of the universities. It involves a high level of engagement and motivation of employees, so that they remain committed to their universities. The leaders of the universities need a clear strategy to:

- Attract and retain the right people.
- Access and grow its human capital.
- Build, maintain and engaged a high-performing workforce.
- Maintain work-life balance.

Attracting and retaining

To attract and retain the right people, universities need to offer its employees workplace options which are flexible enough to meet their needs and changing circumstances. This includes promoting and encouraging diversity in views and opinions without fear of reprisals from university leaders.

This chapter proposes a framework for university sustainability to include the following elements (Fig. 1):

- Diversity
- Democracy

Fig. 1:   Proposed framework for university sustainability.

- Equity
- Quality

Diversity recognises that there are cultural, ethnic and religious differences. University leaders have to understand and accept that within the broader community, there are diverse viewpoints, beliefs and values. The extent to which democracy is exercised in a university reflects how much participation and representation of the relevant stakeholders is allowed by the senior management of the university. The process of decision-making has to be made known and understood by the staff and other stakeholders.

The pressure is on for the university's human resource manager to meet talent needs, manages organisational transformations and identifies talent gaps. An effective workforce with diverse skills and capabilities will

Table 1:   Key attraction and retention drivers in universities.

Attraction Drivers	Retention Drivers
Competitive salary	Competitive compensation
Career advancement	Opportunities to learn and develop new skills and knowledge
Competitive benefits	Satisfaction with organisation's decision
Salary increment due to performance	Employee well-being
Learning and Development opportunities	Decision-making authority/participation in decision-making
Profile of co-workers	Good colleagues
Reputation of university as a good employer	Reputation of university as a caring employer

support the university's goals to capitalise on its strengths and exploit opportunities regarding social and economic sustainability.

University administrators have to understand the key drivers of employee attraction and employee retention (Table 1). Very often, they do not wish to acknowledge the importance of these drivers. Those drivers which relate to "curriculum" and "work environment" determine the extent of "Quality" improvements in the university. Those which relate to "fair compensation", "career advancement" and "learning and development" ensure there are "Equity" and opportunities in the organisation.

"Democracy" gives rise to a certain "decision-making" or "participation in decision-making" within the university environment. Depending on the perception of employees on the importance of each driver, the inability to fulfil these drivers may prompt employees to seek opportunities elsewhere. Employee participation could be in the form of delegation of authority by the supervisor, psychological empowerment and power-sharing.

The concept of Partnership at Work is gaining popularity in many organisations. It calls for consultative arrangements among the various participants of the organisation and encapsulates features such as joint commitment of the parties to ensure success of the organisation, building trust by recognising legitimate roles and interests and addressing the quality of working life.

Assessing and growing human capital

Assessing and growing human capital involves investing in talent development and offering opportunities for career progression. As with any comparable investment, the objective is to maximise value while managing risk. It requires careful planning in line with the university's vision. It also involves providing financial and non-financial support for those pursuing tertiary education or professional qualifications. University leaders need to adopt a management style in accordance with the way the university sees its mission. To create a workforce that shares this vision, university leaders have to gel the team to convey a clear and consistent portrayal of the vision by their words and actions. Huffman and Jacobson (2003) asserted that principals' leadership practices are the best predictor for teachers' participation in change efforts.

Building a high-performance workforce

Building and engaging a high-performing workforce are critical to a university's competitiveness. University leaders have to understand that a high-performance workforce will directly impact the performance of the university. It has to develop and implement a workforce plan which identifies skills and technical expertise needed and actions to meet those skills gaps. Other initiatives may include fostering innovation and creativity, leadership development and succession planning.

Maintaining work-life balance

The university has to adopt a strategy of building a highly-skilled, flexible and high-performing workforce. It can accomplish this by implementing comprehensive benefits and work-life programs. Employees expect employers to recognise that in addition to having a job, they also have a private life. A work-life balance policy reduces the stress employees experience. It enables them to feel that they are paying attention to all important aspects of their lives. Designing an effective work-life balance program will offer the university a competitive advantage in recruiting and retaining staff, increased productivity and increased customer service.

Significance of the study

This study recognises that private university leaders often operate under circumstances that are far from optimal. Very often, they may not understand the multiple complexities and challenges affecting their universities. This chapter proposes a detailed framework focusing on the various elements and components of maintaining sustainability. At the heart of this is the reculturing of the universities. This chapter will add significant new scholarly understanding of and insights into the complex environment of private universities and suggests ways in which implementation can be more structured.

Literature Review

A university's culture can either enhance or impede professional learning. It enhances professional learning when employees believe professional development is important and that this belief and practice pervades throughout the whole organisation. Conversely, negative culture impairs staff development. The culture reflects a shared sense of purpose and values, a commitment to the learning of all students and opportunities for staff reflection and staff inquiry (Stein, 1998; Lambert, 1998; Fullan, 2001; DuFour and Eaker, 1998; Hord, 1998). Fullan (1993) reiterated that change will require a radical reculturing of the school and the redesigning of the teaching profession. Studies have shown that a collaborative culture and teacher participation in decision-making accompanied by transformational leadership are conditions that enhance professional learning and educational change in schools (Sleegers, Geijsel and Van den Berg, 2002; Geijsel, Sleegers, Stoel and Kruger, 2007).

Reculturing is a process of organisational change. Fullan (1993) stated that when reculturing occurs, restructuring follows. Restructuring is not the same as reculturing, as restructuring alters the structure of the organisation and is often non-lasting. Reculturing results in longer lasting reforms (Boyd, 1992). It alters group dynamics and the ability of employees to self-assess and reassess the environment. Staff have to understand the connections between their ideas about existing conditions and the strategies to reform them. It requires a link of culture to structure (Doyle, 1998).

For reculturing to be successful, administrators need to facilitate change in others (Fawcett *et al.*, 2001). That involves engaging staff in discussions that are driven by inquiry and self-reflection. Hargreaves (1994) found that creating structures for collaborations without creating relationships is unproductive. Administrators need to encourage teachers to raise issues and critique unpopular practices and ideologies within the university. Teachers have to experience shared leadership (Huffman and Hipp, 2003) and commitment to the mission and goals of the school (Lee, Smith and Croninger, 1995). There is also a need to have clarity of purpose (DuFour, Eaker and Karhanek, 2004) and commitment to student learning (McLaughlin, 1993; Leithwood, Leonard and Sharatt, 1998).

Spillane (2006) adopted a cognitive perspective when offering the distributed leadership framework as a diagnostic and design tool to help practitioners explore how the practice of leadership is "stretched over" multiple leaders, followers and situation. He suggested that leadership practice is constructed in the interactions between leaders, followers and their situations. Spillane highlights who takes responsibility for a task (he who leads is dictated by the task and not by his hierarchical position) and how the task is accomplished through interactions of multiple leaders and followers. Heck and Hallinger (1999) examined how leaders and others in the organisation create a shared understanding about their role and participation in school.

Ensuring academic freedom is critical to the reculturing efforts of a university. Barnett (1990) argued that academic freedom should be expanded from its narrow definition of staff immunity from censorship towards a universal mandate to present and to criticise ideas. Fessel (2006) urged universities to issue clear statements affirming their commitment to academic freedom and controversial debate. Universities should adopt clear policies supporting academic freedom and steps to deal with challenges to academic freedom in order to support higher order thinking across the campus. Academics should be encouraged to promote critical thinking and have the right to participate in how universities are run without the fear of reprisals from university leaders.

Maintaining staff motivation is a major challenge for university leaders. Research has shown that a positive school culture was associated with increased student motivation and achievement, improved teacher collaboration, and improved attitudes among teachers toward their jobs (Sashkin and Sashkin, 1990; Sashkin and Wahlberg, 1993; Ogawa and Bossert, 1995).

Teachers influence student performance if they are motivated themselves. Teacher quality has a significant impact on student academic performance (Mwamwenda and Mwamwenda, 1989; Lockheed and Verspoor, 1991). More importantly, teacher quality is intertwined with teachers' perception of their work life (Perry, Chapman and Snyder, 1995). Teacher job satisfaction is often regarded as an important determinant on the educational outcomes such as student achievement (Heller, Rex and Cline, 1992; Leslie, 1989).

Raynor (1974) stressed that the higher the expected importance or value of present activities is in relation to future personal goals, the higher is the motivation of individuals and the better is their performance and learning. School management needs to pay particular attention to the way they deal with teachers. Treating teachers with respect, providing good working environment and developing teacher skills and competencies will motivate teachers to perform better. Sirgy (1986) stressed that when the higher order needs such as esteem and self-actualisation needs are met, teachers will move towards a higher level of development. The more motivated the teachers, the greater commitment they will place in their work. When teachers see that their students are progressing and achieving their targets, they become motivated as their esteem needs have been met.

Change can take place at two levels: the organisational level and the individual level (Kotter, 1996; Lewin, 1952; Richardson and Placier, 2001). Change at the organisational level addresses issues such as organisational development and organisational climate. Change at the individual level addresses issues such as motivation, human behaviour and beliefs and the relationship of the impact of these beliefs on the organisation (Richardson and Placier, 2001). Change favours firms that move from static competition towards dynamic improvements and those which are able to create knowledge faster than their competitors (Porter, 1990).

Discussion on Proposed Detailed Framework

This chapter proposes a detailed framework of university sustainability incorporating various elements affecting private universities (Fig. 2).

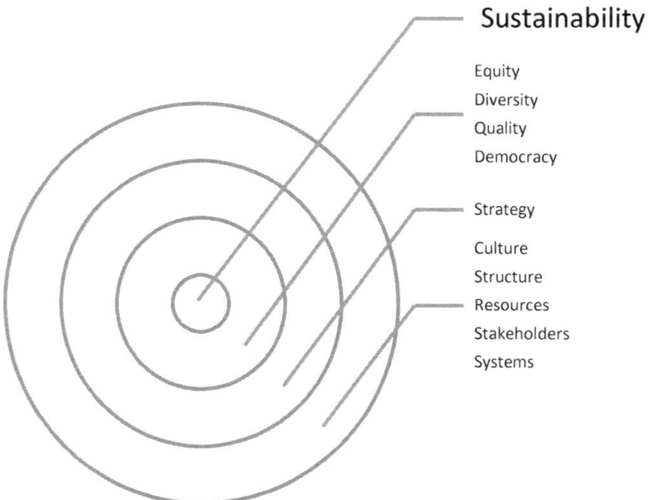

Fig. 2: Detailed framework of sustainability in private universities.

It builds on the core engine comprising Equity, Diversity, Democracy and Quality discussed in Fig. 1 and further incorporates Strategy, Culture, Structure, Stakeholders, Resources, and Systems.

Implementing New Strategies

A private university must reculture to ensure its competitiveness. The concept of competitiveness involves both static and dynamic components. It needs a new paradigm shift to sustain its competitiveness. It must be able to manage its resources and capabilities effectively. Sustainable competitive advantage depends on the core competencies that yield long-term benefits to the university. When the external environment is turbulent and complex, the university has to respond and align with the environment in order to thrive.

The increase in the availability of knowledge online necessitates a fundamental shift in the role of a university. As content is readily available online, teaching methods need to change to focus on contextualisation and student experience. Universities are engines of innovation and sources of new knowledge and ideas. At the same time, university leaders have to demonstrate a large degree of entrepreneurship in the face of competition. Our framework proposes five main components for strategic improvements.

Improved culture

(a) An improved culture would encompass more inclusiveness from various participants. Universities have to encourage and support changes in the way decisions are made. An organisation's capacity for learning determines whether it will thrive or fail (Senge, 1990). Excellence is more likely sustained in organisations that promote continuous collaborative learning rather than in organisations where top–down management approach is the norm. University leaders have to create an atmosphere of change which is conducive to innovation and encourage participation of its employees. Deep and sustained change requires attention over extended period (DuFour, 1999) and may a number of years. Commitment of the university leaders is a must to bring about a sustainable environment for learning. Staff learning is reinforced when they share ideas in faculty meetings and other school activities. Cultures that recognise and support staff learning will bolster a professional learning community.

(b) Barney (2002) proposed linking a company's competitive strategy to performance. The three essential building blocks of high performance business are: (1) market focus and position; (2) distinctive capabilities; and (3) performance anatomy. High-performing businesses all excel at managing five common disciplines: leadership, people development, technology enablement, performance management, and innovation. These five disciplines form the backbone of performance anatomy. Performance anatomy relates to the observable and actionable side of culture which an organisation can actively manage. Applying this performance anatomy concept to private universities, university leaders have to relook at their own leadership styles, the way they interact with employees and their support for innovation.

(c) The other aspects of culture in the performance anatomy framework are hidden and they relate to unwritten rules and collective memories. They may be a hindrance to any change efforts which the university leaders wish to take. The culture of the university has to adapt to the demands of the industry. An adaptive culture allows the fine-tuning of the formal structures, introduce new strategies, and change the leadership styles, yet still inspire the same commitment in its employees. The university's culture needs to be aligned with its strategies and changes in its business environment.

Improved structure

(a) Sustained change can only be accomplished with the commitment of the leader to improve teaching and learning (Schmoker, 2006). A strong professional learning community is oriented to change and its success or failure depends on the commitment, persistence and entrepreneurialism of its leaders. Structural improvements also include capacity enhancement such as motivation, skills, knowledge and support. Adequate capacity is needed if the institution is to carry out reculturing efforts effectively.

Improved access to resources

(a) Private universities need to have access to an enlarged base of funding sources. These could include private as well as public funding in the form of government grants for research activities. Besides looking for new funding resources, university leaders also have to be mindful of competition around them. They have to be receptive to shifting to new market segments or focusing to distant markets that are not focused by the competitors (Gaur, 2007).
(b) The infrastructure of the university, including facilities, is critical in attracting new students to join the institution. Private universities compete aggressively in upgrading their facilities to differentiate themselves from their competitors.
(c) The technological readiness of the university will enhance its productivity and increase its efficiency. Having good information and communication technologies (ICTs) such as campus-wide WIFI access will enhance the learning environment of students and staff. ICT will transform the way education is delivered and supported. New platforms such as online learning will enhance student experience.

Improved systems

(a) The proper management of university finances is critical for ensuring trust in the administration. Indicators capturing the quality of the management of finances should be reviewed periodically to highlight transparency and adherence to accounting standards.

(b) Universities should reduce excessive bureaucracy, red tape and over-regulation, for this will discourage employees from proposing news ideas and initiatives to management.

(c) Universities need to continue to nurture their employees and provide the necessary training and development for skills upgrading. Academics need to learn to develop new curricula which are relevant to the industry before they can impart the knowledge to their students. Changing the university structure or introducing new instructional methods are not enough to alter the core assumptions about teaching and learning. To make a real difference, universities need to reculture their curricula. The promotion of a curricula culture will change the way teachers view curriculum and empower them as curriculum designers.

(d) Learning communities in which teachers meet regularly to talk about their teaching and learning create a structure of continuous improvement for learning and change (Hord, 1997). At the same time, teachers need to be trained on new pedagogical skills as they often lack peer supervision in their work. There is a wide of teaching styles as many teachers have developed teaching strategies that are highly idiosyncratic.

Improved relationships with stakeholders

(a) Companies are looking to collaborate with universities more closely in the areas of research and product development activities. As businesses cut back on their R&D budget, they are increasingly reliant on universities to develop new products. This relationship benefits universities in that students will be able to supplement classroom learning with real-life commercial projects. The quality of a university's business network has a bearing on its competiveness and growth.

(b) Private universities need to attract new talent into their workforce. They have to study new models as the needs and aspirations of academics have changed. World-class universities are characterised by a high concentration of excellence and talent. They embrace diversity rather than homogeneity in their talent pool. The increase in integration and coordination of diverse talents creates opportunities for pedagogical reculturing and new learning relationships.

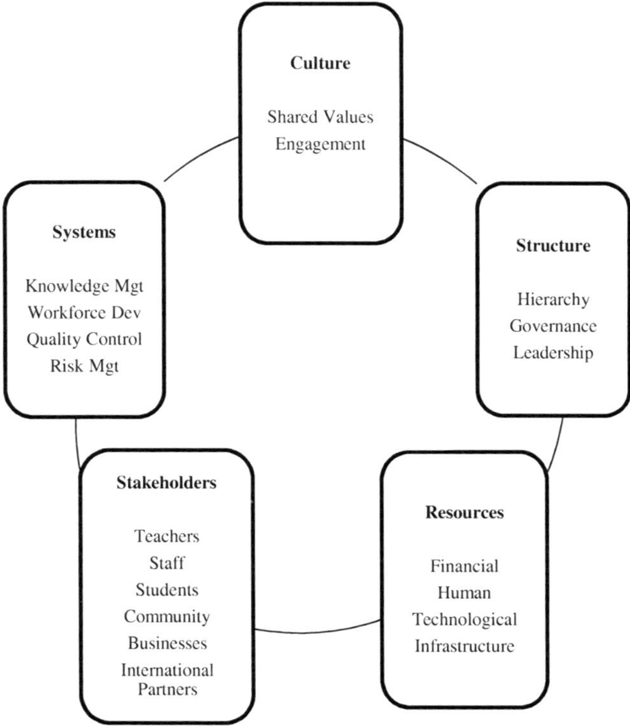

Fig. 3:   Detailed version of outer ring of framework.

(c) Students need to know the various options available for them, including the multiple entry and exit points, the career prospects and the range of curricular activities. For example, they would like to know if the university has dual degree partnership arrangements with foreign universities. The university needs to foster diversity in its student population in order to promote cross-cultural and international awareness. Universities also need to embrace life-long learning in their curriculum as working adults may return to the university to upgrade their skills and increase their chances of finding work in the area of their training. (Strosnider, 1998). At the same time, universities should not ignore students' non-academic outcomes such as students' involvement in student governance and their understanding of their empowerment and personal identity.

Conclusion

The five components in our proposed detailed framework for sustainability of private universities are not independent. They are highly intertwined and tend to reinforce each other. Universities need clear and strong cultures to foster professional learning. When universities have strong positive cultures, staff and student learning thrive. Conversely, negative cultures can impair staff development. Teachers and staff professional development and quality curriculum are the keys to successful reculturing of universities. University leaders must develop cooperative relationships with employees to build a strong learning community. With strong cultures of trust, openness and collaboration that support both students and staff learning, private universities will be able to sustain high performance and remain competitive in the long run.

The proposed framework in this chapter has both theoretical and practical significance. It presents a detailed theoretical framework for private universities as learning institution. University leaders should not lose focus on the four elements discussed in Fig. 1 that determine the universities sustainability. In addition, the proposed five components for strategic improvements elaborated in Fig. 2 will position them more competitively in the face of growing demands from students and staff. The practical contribution of this chapter emphasises the necessary actions university leaders must take to ensure a sustainable institution.

References

Barney, J.B. (2002). *Gaining and sustaining competitive advantage.* New Jersey: Prentice Hall.

Barnett, R. (1990). The Idea of Higher Education. Buckingham, UK: Open University Press.

Barnett, R. (2004). Learning for an unknown future. *Higher Education Research & Development,* **23**(3), 247–260.

Boyd, W. (1992). The power of paradigms: Reconceptualizing policy and management. *Educational Administration Quarterly,* **29**, 504–528.

Coaldrake, P., and Stedman, L. (1999). *Academic work in the twenty-first century: Changing roles and policies.* Occasional Papers Series (pp. 1–35). Canberra: Australian Department of Education, Training and Youth Affairs.

Doyle, L.H. (1998). *The overlap of perspective in leadership, teaching, organization, and context*. Paper presented at the American Education Research Asociation, San Diego, CA.

DuFour, R. (1999). *Help wanted: Principals who can lead professional communities*. National Association of Secondary School, *Principals Bulletin*, **83**(604), 12–17.

DuFour, R., Eaker, R., DuFour, R., and Karhanek, G. (2004). *Whatever it takes: How professional learning communities respond when kids don't learn*. Bloomington, IN: National Educational Service.

DuFour, R., and Eaker, R. (1998). *Professional learning communities at work: Best practices for enhancing student achievement*. Bloomington, Ind.: National Educational Service.

Fawcett, G., Brobeck, D., Andrews, S., and Walker, L. (2001). Principals and beliefs-driven change. *Phi Delta Kappan*, **82**(5), 405–410.

Fessel, S. (2006). The impact of academic freedom policies on critical thinking instruction. Insight: *A Collection of Faculty Scholarship*, **1**, 51–58.

Fullan, M. (1993). *Change forces*. Philadelphia: The Falmer Press.

Fullan, M. (2001). *Leading in a culture of change*. San Francisco: Jossey-Bass.

Fulmer, R.M., Gibbs, P.A., and Goldsmith, M. (2000). Developing leaders: How winning companies keep on winning. *Sloan Management Review*, Fall, pp. 49–59.

Gaur, A.S. (2007), *Essays on strategic adaptation and firm performance during institutional transition*, doctoral dissertation, National University of Singapore.

Geijsel, F.P., Sleegers, P.J.C., Stoel, R., and Krüger, M.L. (2007). *The effect of psychological, organizational and leadership factors on professional learning in schools*. Paper presented at the annual meeting of the American Educational Research Association (AERA), Chicago, 9–13 April.

Hanna, D.E. (2003). Building a leadership vision: Eleven strategic challenges for higher education. *Educause*, July–August, pp. 25–34.

Hargreaves, A. (1994). *Changing teachers, changing times: Teachers work and culture in the postmodern age*. London: Cassell.

Hargreaves, A. (2003). Teaching in the knowledge society. New York: Teachers College Press.

Heck, G., and Hallinger. P. (1999). Next generation methods for the study of leadership and school improvement. In Murphy, J. and Seashore Louis, K. (Eds.), *Handbook of research on educational administration*, (2nd edn.). (pp. 141–162). San Francisco, CA: Jossey Bass Publishers.

Heller, H., Rex, J.C., and Cline, M.P. (1992). Factors Related to Teachers Job Satisfaction and Dissatisfaction. *ERS Spectrum*, **10**(1), 20–24.

Hord, S.M. (1997). *Professional learning communities: Communities of continuous inquiry and improvement.* Austin, TX: Southwest Educational Development Library.

Hord, S.M. (1998). *Creating a professional learning community: Cottonwood Creek School.* Washington, DC: Office of Educational Research and Improvement. (ERIC Document Reproduction No. ED424685).

Huffman, J.B., and Hipp, K.K. (Eds.), (2003). *Reculturing schools as professional learning communities.* Lanham, MD: Scarecrow Publishing.

Knight, P.T., and Trowler, P.R. (2000). Department level cultures and the improvement of learning and teaching. *Studies in Higher Education,* **25**, 69–83.

Huffman, J.B. and Jacobson, A.L. (2003). Perceptions of professional learning communities. *International Journal of Leadership in Education,* **6**(3), 239–250.

Kotter, J. (1996). *Leading change.* Boston, MA: Harvard Business School Press.

Lee, V.E., Smith, J.B., and Croninger, R.G. (1995), *Another Look at High School Restructuring. Issues in Restructuring Schools,* Report No. 9, Center on Organization and Restructuring of Schools (CORS), Wisconsin University.

Leithwood, K., Leonard, L. and Sharratt, L. (1998). Conditions fostering organizational learning in schools. *Educational Administration Quarterly,* **35**, 679–706.

Leslie, K. (1989). Administrators Must Consider and Improve Teacher Satisfaction. *NASSP Bulletin,* **73**, 19–22.

Lewin, K. (1952). *Field theory in social science.* London: Tavistock.

Lingard, B., Hayes, D., Mills, M., and Christie, P. (2003). *Leading learning.* Philadephia: Open University Press.

Lockheed, M., and Vespoor, A. (1991). *Improving Primary Education in Developing Countries.* Oxford: Oxford University Press.

Longden, B. (2006). An institutional response to changing student expectations and their impact on retention rates. *Journal of Higher Education Policy and Management,* **28**(2), 173–187.

McLaughlin, M.W. (1993). What matters most in teachers' workplace context? In Little, J.W., and McLaughlin, M.W. (Eds.), *Teachers' work: Individuals, colleagues, and contexts* (pp. 79–103). New York: Teachers College Press.

Meek, V. L., and Wood, F. Q. (1997). *Higher education government and management: An Australian study.* Evaluations and Investigations Program, Higher Education Division, Department of Employment, Education, Training and Youth Affairs. January. Retrieved September 13, 2003, from http://www.detya.gov.au/archive/ highered/eippubs/eip9701/front.htm.

Mwamwenda, T.S., and Mwmwenda, B.B. (1989). Teacher Characteristics and Pupils' Academic Achievemen in Botswana Primary Education. *International Journal of Educational Development,* **9**(1), 31–42.

Ogawa, R., and Bossert, S. (1995). Leadership as an organizational quality. *Educational Administration Quarterly*, **31**, 224–243.

Perry, P., Chapman, D., and Snyder, C. (1995). Quality of teacher worklife and classroom practices in Botswana. *International Journal of Educational Development*, **15**(2), 115–125.

Porter, M.E. (1990). *The Competitive Advantage of Nations*. Macmillan, London.

Pratt, G., and Poole, D. (1999). Globalisation and Australian universities, policies and impacts. *International Journal of Public Sector Management*, **12**(6), 533–544.

Ramsden, P. (1998). Managing the effective University. *Higher Education Research and Development*, **17**(3), 347–370.

Raynor, J.O. (1974) Relationships between achievement-related motives, future orientation, and academic performances, in: Atkinson, J.W., and Taynor, J.O. (Eds.), *Motivation and Achievement,* pp. 121–154 (Washington DC, Winston).

Richardson, V., and Placier, P. (2001). *Teacher change. Handbook of research on teaching* (pp. 905–947). Washington, DC: American Educational Research Association.

Sashkin, M., and Sashkin, M. (1990). *Leadership and culture building in schools: Quantitative and qualitative understandings.* Paper presented at the annual meeting of the American Educational Research Association, Boston, MA.

Sashkin, M., and Walberg, H.J. (1993). *Educational leadership and school culture.* Berkeley, CA: McCutchan Publishing Corporation.

Schmoker, M. (2006). *Results now: How we can achieve unprecedented improvements in teaching and learning.* Alexandria, VA: Association for Supervision and Curriculum Development.

Senge, P.M. (1990). *The fifth discipline: The art and practice of the learning organization.* New York: Currency Double Day.

Sirgy, M.J. (1986). A Quality-of-Life Theory Derived from Maslow's Developmental Perspective. *American Journal of Economics and Sociology*, **45**(3), 328–342.

Sleegers, P., Geijsel, F., and Dan Berg, R.V. (2002). *Second International Handbook of Educational Leadership and Administration*, pp. 75–102, Leithwood, K. and Hallinger, P. (Eds.), Dordrecht: Kluwer Academic Publisher.

Spillane, J. (2006). *Distributed leadership.* San Francisco, CA: Jossey Bass.

Stein, M. (1998). *High performance learning communities District 2: Report on Year One implementation of school learning communities. High performance training communities project.* Washington, DC: Office of Educational Research and Improvement. (ERIC Document Reproduction No. ED429263).

Strosnider, K. (1998). For-profit higher education sees booming enrolments and revenues. *The Chronicle of Higher Education*, p. A36.

Snyder, H., Marginson, S., and Lewis, T. (2007). An alignment of the planets: Mapping the intersections between pedagogy, technology and management in Australian universities. *Journal of Higher Education Policy and Management,* **29**(2), 1–16.

Yu, S.O. (2009). Principal Leadership for Private Schools Improvement: The Singapore Perspective. *The Journal of International Social Research,* **2**(6), 714–749.

視人之國若視其國, 視人之家若視其家, 視人之身若視其身

They look at the states of others as if they were their own states; they look at the families of others as if they were their own families; they look at others as if they were themselves.

Mozi

Chapter 5

Reevaluating Teaching Effectiveness

This chapter aims to explore the differences in the feedback scores of lecturers evaluated by diploma and degree students in a private university in Malaysia. Currently, all students evaluate lecturers teaching at both the diploma and degree levels using the same set of questionnaires. As the entry requirements for the two classes of students are different, the feedback results do not fully reflect the teaching efficiency of the lecturers. An upward reweighting of the feedback scores of Diploma level lecturers to ensure more parity in the teacher evaluation process was proposed. The University's human resource policies need to be fine-tuned to take into consideration the differences between the two classes of students. The current system of not revealing the various component scores of the feedback process to the lecturers is counter-productive as lecturers do not know which aspects of their teaching need to be improved and which aspects are appreciated by students. For the feedback process to be effective, lecturers need to receive timely and substantive information about their performance.

Introduction

The effectiveness of the evaluation process depends largely on the proper design and assessment of the evaluation criteria. Successful feedback mechanisms demand attention to identifying competencies of actors such as lecturers as well as developing evaluation criteria specific to different groups of respondents such as students. Lecturers often expressed frustrations about the mechanisms of the teacher evaluation process by students. The timing of the feedback process in the first half of the semester did not give sufficient time for both lecturers and students to know each other well. Lecturers need time to engage the students fully to understand their learning needs and capabilities while students require time to adapt to the teaching styles of lecturers. Feedback has to be given as soon as possible when the learning task is completed to allow lecturers to internalise the feedback findings and make any changes to their teaching styles. The current system of not revealing the various component scores of the feedback process to the lecturers is counter-productive as lecturers do not know which aspects of their teaching need to be improved and which aspects are appreciated by students. For the feedback process to be effective, lecturers need to receive timely and substantive information about their performance. The absence in providing these outcomes will result in concerns among lecturers that the appraisal process is just an administrative exercise which does not fully reflect their competencies.

Human resource policies need to be adjusted to give considerable attention to sound procedures to assess performance against certain standards. The evaluation process has to be both measurable and reliable. The current lecturer evaluation process is unreliable as it does not take into account the differences in academic standing between diploma and degree level students. The entry requirements into a diploma programme are lower than a degree program. Students entering into a degree-level program have two additional years of high school education as compared to those enrolling in a diploma-level program.

This section proposes a conceptual framework which integrates formative assessment and summative assessment. The formative assessment methods that lecturers use to conduct evaluations of students comprehension and academic progress help to validate the summative assessment of teaching which are recorded as feedback scores of teachers. Combining both student improvement and accountability functions into a comprehensive lecturer evaluation process requires an adjustment in human resource policies.

Table 1:   Entry requirements.

Diploma	Equivalent of 3 "O Level" subjects
Degree	Equivalent of "A Level" or Diploma

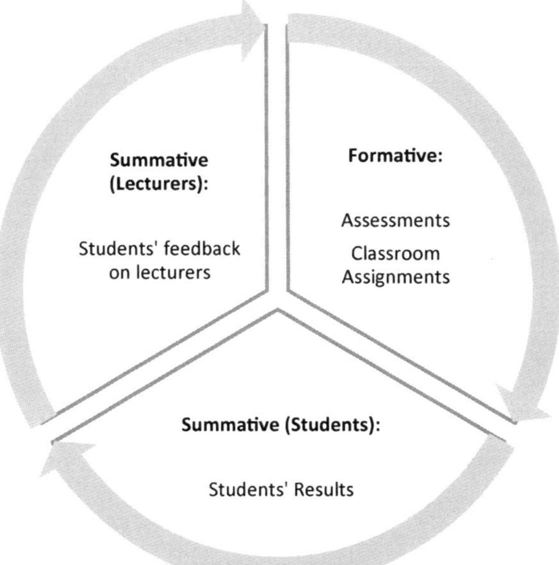

Fig. 1:   General conceptual framework.

The traditional approach to teacher evaluation process is formative in nature. The formative assessment monitors student learning to provide ongoing feedback that can be used by lecturers to improve their teaching, and by students to improve their learning. Summative assessment evaluates student learning at the end of an instructional unit through examination or a final project. Our framework combines an element of summative assessment of lecturers by students through the use of student evaluation questionnaire (Fig. 1).

More importantly, research studies have shown that gains in student achievement are also attributed to other factors such as school environment, school culture and individual student needs and motivation (Yu, 2016).

Significance of the Study

This study recognises that lecturers' evaluation by students is part of the overall assessment of lecturers' performance. Universities often use questionnaires as a student feedback tool. However, universities failed to differentiate the academic standing of the classes of students responding to the questionnaires. This chapter stresses that the differences in feedback responses by diploma and degree students are due to the different academic standings of the two classes of students. University administrators should re-examine the feedback processes for the different classes of respondents in relation to its effectiveness in improving the teaching and learning outcomes of both lecturers and students.

Literature Review

Student feedback is one of the most common tool which influences learning and achievement. Research by Natriello (1987) and Crooks (1988) have found that substantial learning gains could be achieved when teachers introduced formative assessment into their classroom practice. Formative assessment relates to assessment to generate feedback on performance to improve and accelerate learning (Sadler, 1998). Black and William (1998) noted that student feedback produced significant benefits in learning and achievement across all content areas, knowledge and levels of education.

Feedback can only be effective if it is understood and internalised by students before it can be used to make improvements. Very often, students do not understand the importance of the feedback given by teachers, and therefore are not able to fully comprehend the intentions of teachers and the effects they would like to produce (Chanock, 2000). To overcome this situation, teachers should engage in constant dialogue with students to develop their understanding of expectations and standards. Butler (1987) noted that grading student performance has less effect than giving feedback as students tend to compare their grades with their peers rather than focusing on ways to improve their tasks.

Good feedback helps teachers to improve their performance (Yorke, 2003). Teachers need good information about how their students are progressing so that they can refine their teaching accordingly. An effective feedback mechanism facilitates the development of self-assessment (reflection) in learning as well as encourages positive motivational beliefs and self-esteem (Nicol and Macfarlane-Dick, 2006). Tram and Williamson

(2009) noted two approaches in the evaluation of teaching: teaching-focused and learning-focused. Teaching-focused evaluation emphasises the course content, activities and teaching techniques as well as the characteristics of teachers. Learning-focused evaluation, on the other hand, focused on the effectiveness of the teachers to improve student learning. It measures student expectations, their perceptions of the learning environment and the appropriateness of the learning activities. Hajdin and Pazur (2012) concluded that teacher and teaching effectiveness should be evaluated separately. Studies by Hattie and Timperley (2007) noted that quality feedback has significant impact on student learning achievements. Most improvements in student learning were recorded when students receive feedback about how to do a task effectively. They also found that learning achievement is low when feedback focuses on "praise, rewards and punishments". It is most effective when the goals are measurable and achievable. Universities should focus on how appraisal and feedback systems improve students performance. Measures should be developed to assess the effectiveness of the feedback process and this include informing lecturers of the benchmarks against which performance is assessed. Yu (2016) noted that universities need to reculture to remain sustainable and that positive culture will facilitate staff and student learning.

Establishing a classroom environment that facilitates learning requires special skills from teachers. Swartz *et al.* (1990) assessed teacher performance on five functions: instructional presentations, instructional monitoring, instructional feedback, management of time and management of students behaviour. Yu (2016) concluded that student achievement has a strong effect on teacher motivation. The higher the student achievement, the more motivated are the teachers. Teachers are motivated when they feel that their contribution will be appreciated (Yu, 2012).

Developing a comprehensive teacher evaluation tool is challenging. Isore (2009) noted that there are costs involved at every stage of the process, from consultations with relevant stakeholders to reaching agreements. Danielson (1996, 2007) stressed the high costs and time of training evaluators. Heneman *et al.* (2006) indicated the unwillingness of teachers and evaluators to take on additional workload unless other workloads and responsibilities are reduced.

Research by Shin *et al.* (2006) comparing the critical thinking ability of undergraduate nursing students provided evidence that bachelor degree students scored higher on critical thinking than associate degree and diploma students. The study concluded that the length and content of the educational program is important for encouraging students to develop their critical thinking abilities earlier.

Research Question

We began with several key questions:
(1) Are there differences in feedback scores of Diploma and Degree level students?
(2) What could possibly be the main reason for the differences, if any?

Methodology

The main goal of the research was to highlight the differences in the response rate between diploma and degree-level students. The research study was conducted on students of the Faculty of Business over a two semester period. The sample included 30 lecturers who taught at both diploma and degree levels. A total of 30 different diploma and 30 degree subjects per semester were chosen. There were 1,100 student participants in the survey. The class size per level ranged from 10 to 80 students per class. The research was based on one online survey exercise per semester in the form of a questionnaire administered by the Registry department.

A typical four-point ordinal Likert scale was used by the respondent to rate the degree of teaching effectiveness. Both the diploma and degree level students were given the same questionnaire to measure the attitudes or opinions under investigation.

The students were asked to fill up an online survey form which consisted of 25 questions (Appendix 1). Survey respondents were asked to give their views on how much they agreed with the statements relating to delivery of curriculum, student support, classroom management and utilisation of e-learning. No incentives were provided for the participants and their participation was compulsory. The responses to the questionnaires were compiled by the Registry office and an overall feedback score was tabulated for each lecturer. The feedback scores were analysed using the IBM SPSS statistical software package.

The one-way analysis of variance (ANOVA) was used to determine Research Question 1 on whether there were any significant differences between the mean scores of the two classes of students. Research Question 2 is descriptive in nature and relates to the entry requirements of the Diploma and Degree students.

Results and Discussions

Table 2 shows the differences in the mean for the two groups of students. The Diploma class is denoted by "1" while the Degree class is denoted by "2" The mean score of respondents in Diploma programs (78.87) is lower than those in Degree programs (81.87). We use a 95% confidence interval for the dependent variable "score". The differences in the mean scores are most likely due to the different academic standing of the two classes of respondents. Students who have not met the entry requirements for the Degree program are enrolled in Diploma programs. Degree-level students are those who have either met the entry requirements or have graduated from a Diploma level program. In general, degree-level students have two additional years of high school education.

Table 2:   Descriptive statistics.

	N	Minimum	Maximum	Mean	Std. Deviation
Diploma	60	51.75	91.50	78.8757	7.76433
Degree	60	51.00	97.00	81.8780	6.44937
Valid N (listwise)	60				

Table 3:   *ANOVA* score.

	Sum of Squares	df	Mean Square	F	Sig.
Between Groups	270.420	1	270.420	5.309	0.023
Within Groups	6010.869	118	50.940		
Total	6281.289	119			

The output of the ANOVA analysis showed a significance level of 0.023 ($p = 0.023$). This is below the 0.05 significance level and, therefore, we can conclude that there is a statistically significant difference in the mean score between the two classes of students.

Student performance measures such as test scores and assessments form an important parameter of our framework. It occurs at the summative evaluation stage which is normally during the mid-term and final term exam period. It can be used as a diagnostic tool to assess students learning and this has implications on teaching efficiency. The above findings gave evidence of the importance of promoting "Critical Thinking" as a compulsory subject rather than as an elective subject currently. It is essential for universities to define the objectives that encourage students critical thinking abilities and to develop curriculum and teaching methodologies to meet these objectives. The evaluation of teaching activities is important as it ensures the quality of teaching and student learning. Different procedures are carried out to evaluate the training objectives and competencies of lecturers in delivering teaching activities to students. While the key elements in the evaluation model may be applicable to both diploma and degree-level students, the quantitative evaluation in the form of feedback score needs to be adjusted for those lecturers teaching diploma-level courses.

Student feedback is only one component of evaluating teacher teaching effectiveness. Other measures such as student achievement, content knowledge, instructional planning and delivery, and classroom management are equally important (Fig. 2).

Recommendations

Universities need to re-compute the overall feedback score of diploma-level lecturers through an upward reweighting of the overall score. From the results of our analysis, the mean differences range from 1.8% to 5.9% taking into consideration the standard deviations of both means. Conservatively, we would recommend a 3% reweighting upwards in the feedback scores of lectures teaching diploma-level subjects to make them more comparable to those teaching degree-level courses. The Adjusted Feedback Scores (AFS) is represented by the equation below: Adjusted Feedback Scores (AFS) of diploma-level lecturers = 1.03 × initial feedback score.

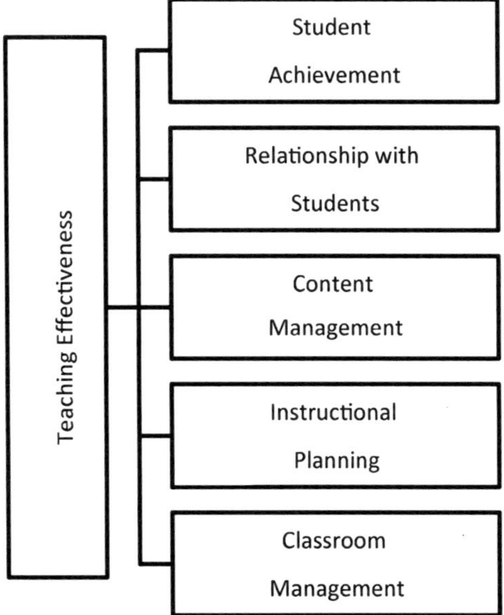

Fig. 2:   Components of teaching effectiveness.

The multiplier of 1.03 takes into account the different academic standings of the two classes of students and ensures more parity in the teacher evaluation processes between diploma and degree-level lecturers.

The ongoing process of improving professional teaching is essential for ensuring student learning success and this has to be the main focus of the evaluation process. Our proposed framework recommends that the university incorporates the following elements in a new lecturer appraisal and feedback system (Fig. 3). These include:

(a) Student performance.
(b) Student assessment of lecturers.
(c) Peer observation of classroom teaching.
(d) Peer collaboration.
(e) Self-assessment, reflection and planning.
(f) Introducing Critical Thinking as a compulsory subject at diploma-level.
(g) The feedback exercise to be held in the second half of the semester.

The purpose of lecturer evaluation needs to be conveyed clearly to students. Both lecturers and students need to know what aspects of

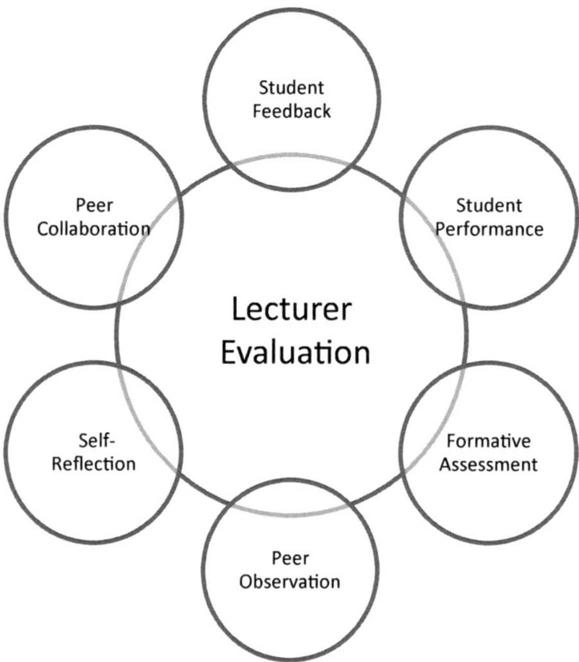

Fig 3: Proposed conceptual framework for differentiated teacher evaluation.

lecturer evaluation are monitored. At the same time, the outcomes objectives, performance indicators and reference standards should be make known by the human resource department to the lecturers. Specific goals are more meaningful than general ones as they help to focus on students achievements and feedback. They also assist to reduce the gap between actual and desired levels of performance. Lecturers' professional profiles, including specialised knowledge and skills should be listed clearly and measured against reference standards which are made known to lecturers. The accountability function of lecturer evaluation holds lecturers accountable for their performance. The outcome of good feedback should result in some form of recognition and reward for it to be effective. Conversely, poor feedback may result in some kind of sanctions against the lecturer. This policy has to be transparent to lecturers to avoid any feeling of demotivation or disgruntlement. University leaders have the ability to motivate teachers and must create an environment that promotes change (Yu, 2009). They should encourage the use of the feedback process as a legitimate tool for lecturer development and avoid any unnecessary bureaucratic procedures associated with the reward mechanism. Our proposed conceptual framework includes "Critical Thinking" as a compulsory subject rather than an elective subject to develop the critical thinking skills of all students. For the evaluation feedback to be effective, the timing of the feedback exercise should be moved to the second half of the semester to enable students to adapt to the teaching styles of lecturers. The present system of not revealing to the lecturers the components of the feedback scores needs to be changed, as lecturers are unaware which aspects of their teaching need improvement. Only through a comprehensive understanding of their teaching capabilities and inadequacies can they improve their performance.

References

Black, P., and Wiliam, D. (1998). Assessment and classroom learning, *Assessment in Education*, **5**(1), 7–74.

Butler, R. (1987). Task-involving and ego-involving properties of evaluation: effects of different feedback conditions on motivational perceptions, interest and performance, *Journal of Educational Psychology*, **78**(4), 210–216.

Chanock, K. (2000). Comments on essays: do students understand what tutors write? *Teaching in Higher Education*, **5**(1), 95–105.

Crooks, T.J. (1988). The impact of classroom evaluation practices on students, *Review of Educational Research*, **58**(4), 438–481.

Danielson, C. (1996, 2007). *Enhancing Professional Practice: a Framework for Teaching*, (1st and 2nd edn.), Association for Supervision and Curriculum Development (ASCD), Alexandria, Virginia.

Hajdin, G., and Pazur, K. (2012). Differentiating between students evaluation of teacher and teaching effectiveness. *Journal of Informational and Organizational Sciences*, **36**(2), 123–134.

Hattie, J., and Timperley, H. (2007). The Power of feedback. *Review of Educational Research*, **77**, 81–112.

Heneman, H., Milanowski, A., Kimball, S., and Odden, A. (2006). *Standards-Based Teacher Evaluation as a Foundation for Knowledge- and Skill-Based Pay*, Consortium for Policy Research in Education (CPRE) Policy Briefs RB-45.

Isoré, M. (2009). *Teacher Evaluation: Current Practices in OECD Countries and a Literature Review*, OECD Education Working Paper No. 23, OECD, Paris. Available from www.oecd.org/edu/workingpapers.

Natriello, G. (1987). The impact of evaluation processes on students, *Educational Psychologist*, **22**(2), 155–175.

Nicol, D.J., and Macfarlane-Dick, D. (2006). Formative assessment and self-regulated learning: A model and seven principles of good feedback practice, *Studies in Higher Education*, 31(2), 199–218, doi:10.1080/03075070600572090.

Sadler, D.R. (1998). Formative assessment: Revisiting the territory, *Assessment in Education*, 5(1), 77–84.

Shin, S., Ha, J., Shin, K., and Davis, M. (2006). Critical thinking ability of associate, baccalaureate and RN-BSN senior students in Korea. *Journal of Nursing*, **26**(9), 354–361.

Swartz, C.W., White, K.P., Stuck G.B., and Patterson, T. (1990). The Factorial Structure of the North Carolina teaching performance appraisal instruments. *Educational and Psychological Measurement*, **50**, 175–182.

Tram, D.N., and Williamson, J. (2009). *Evaluation of teaching: hidden assumptions about conception of teaching*, Proceedings of the 2nd International Conference of Teaching and Learning (ITCL), INTI University College, Malaysia.

Yorke, M. (2003). Formative assessment in higher education: moves towards theory and the enhancement of pedagogic practice, *Higher Education*, **45**(4), 477–501.

Yu, S.O. (2009). Principal leadership for private schools improvement: The Singapore perspective. *The Journal of International Social Research*, **2**(6), 714–749.

Yu, S.O. (2012). Complexities of multiple paradigms in higher education leadership today. *Journal of Global Management*, **4**(1), 92–100.

Yu, S.O. (2016). Conundrum of Private Schools in Singapore. *International Journal of Business and General Management*, 5(3), 37–64.

Yu, S.O. (2016). Reculturing: The key to sustainability of private universities. *International Journal of Education and Research*, **4**(3), 353–366.

務民之義、敬鬼神而遠之。可謂知矣

To give one's self earnestly to the duties due to men, and, while respecting spiritual beings, to keep aloof from them, may be called wisdom.

Confucius, Analects

Chapter 6

Remaking the University as an Institution of Choice

This chapter uses the metaphor of University Remodelling as a framework for analysing students' choice of a private university and repositioning the university through rebranding of its professors. Remodelling the university involves reconstructing competencies and strengths of the institution. These elements are critical to the growth of the university. Managing growth requires understanding of the factors influencing students' choice of a university, institutional commitment towards improving these factors, and rebranding the university to differentiate itself from its competitors. The creation of a strong university brand is a strategic issue that requires close collaboration between university administrators and academicians, and should not be left to the marketing department alone.

Introduction

Most traditional universities need to rebrand themselves to seize opportunities or to thwart potential threats in the future. Proactive rebranding is necessary in response to expected growth and partnership opportunities. A rebranding exercise is essential for the university to appeal to a new audience which is increasingly more demanding and knowledgeable. Rebranding may not necessarily require an actual name change or logo change. It has to create an impact that competitors take note of. The exercise should help the university regain the foothold which it has lost and to give it a new facelift to react to competition. Rebranding necessitates a new way of running the business. Appealing to a wider customer base require careful planning of marketing and promotional activities, and targeting the services and product offerings across a wide market segment. Effective product positioning requires a clear understanding of the customer needs so that proper communication channels are chosen to convey the message across to them. The marketing plan has to identify the key elements that differentiate the university from its competitors' product offerings. University administrators need to understand the drivers that influence students and see how these drivers could be implemented to attract more students.

University programmes should be aligned with the economic needs of the society. This means that the programmes offered are relevant and meeting the demands of employers. While some universities may choose to be teaching universities and others to be research universities, the key to becoming a "university of excellence" is the reputation of its professors.

Rebranding of professors is a message that distinguishes the university from its competitor. It entails change not only in the identity of the university but also leads to change within the university. It will facilitate change of perceptions of the image among external stakeholders such as students, businesses and government. The exercise may incur investments in professors to participate in more conferences and conduct research projects. The university could build its brand name around a small core group of distinguished professors.

Capitalising on skilled talent will help the university drive innovation and customer value. The branding of professors not only showcases the talents of the university but also gives the impression that the university is serious about investing in human capital and knowledge management. The concept of competency branding shows and markets the university's capabilities in certain fields where distinguished academicians add their market values to the organisation. Employee branding and positioning are closely linked when customers perceive that employees are closely connected to the product offerings.

Our proposed framework consists of four elements of remodelling (Fig. 1). The four elements are: (1) structure; (2) culture; (3) rebranding; and (4) growth strategies. This chapter will focus more on rebranding and growth strategies as key elements to attract and recruit students to the university. The elements of Organisational Structure and Culture have been discussed by Yu (2016) in a paper entitled "Reculturing: The key to sustainability of private universities".

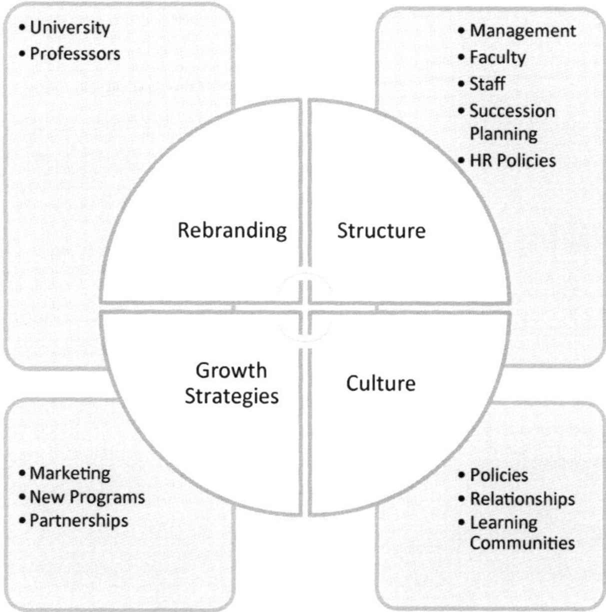

Fig. 1:   Elements of remodelling.

Literature Review

Choosing a university is a difficult choice. Hossler and Gallagher (1987) suggested a three phase model which showed that at every level, the interaction between individual and organisational factors produces outcomes which affect students' choice.

The first phase is the "predisposition" phase where a student's decisions are affected by his ability, his achievement in high school, his socioeconomic status, parents, peer, education and school activities (Tillerry, 1973; Litten, 1982; Stage and Hossler, 1989; Somers *et al.*, 1999).

The second stage involves him finding out more information about the university and formulating a choice about the group of institutions to which he wishes to apply. This second stage is called the "search" phase and is affected by his initial search activities about the university (Chapman, 1981; Hossler and Gallahgher, 1987).

The final phase is making the choice. Factors to consider include educational and occupational aspirations, costs and financial aid, and university courtship activities (Hossler and Gallagher, 1987; John, 1990).

The economic and sociologic theoretical frameworks have been widely used to examine factors of college choice (Hearn, 1984; Tierney, 1983; Somers, Haines and Keene, 2006). These frameworks focus on three approaches to modelling college choice: (a) economic models, (b) status-attainment models; and (c) combined models.

The economic model focus on the assumptions that students think rationally and consider the costs and benefits when choosing a college (Hossler, Smith and Vesper, 1999). The status-attainment model states that students consider a variety of social and individual factors leading to educational aspirations (Jackson, 1982). The combined model considers both the economic models and status-attainment models. An important consideration for most students and parents is education costs. Cabrera and La Nasa (2000) noted that tuition increase is negatively correlated with enrolment. Receiving financial aid is more important than the amount of aid received because providing aid sends a signal that the institution wants students to be part of its community (Jackson, 1982; Abrahamson and Hossler, 1990). Foskett *et al.* (2006) concluded that having flexibility in paying fees, availability of financial aid, and reasonable accommodation costs exert a significant influence on students' choice of the institution.

Houston (1979); Krone *et al.* (1983); Webb (1993) observed that programmed related issues such as length of the programme and entry requirements were the most important consideration to the students in choosing a university. Krampf and Heinlein (1981) found that students compared programmes offered by various institutions to check their suitability.

The availability of majors also influences the choice of institution (Choy and Ottinger 1998; Hossler *et al.*, 1999). Entry requirements are viewed more importantly than the programme offerings (Bourke, 2000; Brennan, 2001).

Litten (1980), Tierney (1983) and Seneca and Taussig (1987) noted that academically-talented students evaluated their choice of university based on the quality of programmes while average students focused on factors such as physical facilities and social life. Facilities such as library, computer rooms, study areas all constitute important elements in students' decision-making process (Qureshi, 1995; Price *et al.*, 2003). Students characteristics such as academic ability, educational aspirations, courses attended during high school and high school achievement all have influences over students' choice of institution (Chapman, 1981; Cabera and La Nasa, 2000).

The location of the university is an important element in students decision-making process. Jackson (1982) stressed that students generally consider institutions nearer to their homes that present no extra financial burdens.

The reputation of the institution has a significant impact on students choice (Kotler and Fox, 1995). Higher education institutions need to differentiate themselves from their competitors (Paramewaran and Glowacka, 1995). Together, good quality and efficient branding, are important elements to attract students to the institution (Hall, 1993; Qureshi, 1995; Bourke, 2000). The academic reputation and prestige of the institution facilitate students' decision-making in choosing an institution (Krampf and Heinlein, 1981; Lin, 1997; Soutar and Turner, 2002). Branding in human resource is the concept of promoting the organisational capabilities. Employee branding facilitates the internalisation of desired brand image and motivates the employees to project that image to customers (Miles and Mangold, 2004). A brand has a significant influence on the selection of a university in the highly competitive education sector (Mourad *et al.*, 2011; Chen, 2008).

Providing good and relevant information to students will assist students in their choice of institution (Cleopatra *et al.*, 2004). The information could include career prospects of the courses studied and the likelihood of securing a job within a year of graduation. Joseph and Joseph (1998, 2000) reiterated that information about course and career prospects are the most important factors during students' selection process. Students' interactions with teachers during the counselling session on Open Days have an impact on their decision-making in choosing an institution. Teacher enthusiasms can be observed in two different ways (Kunter *et al.*, 2011); first, the behavioural approach observed from gestures, tone, or facial expr. (Collins, 1978; Sanders and Gosenpud, 1986); the second manifests the internal experiences of teacher enthusiasms for teaching (Kunter *et al.*, 2011). Studies by Chapman (1986) showed that high school personnel had a significant influence in students' choice process. In addition, family, friends, peers, teachers and counsellors all have a certain degree of influence over students' decisions (Stefanie, 2006). Leslie *et al.* (1977) found that students are most likely to rely in their high school counsellor. They see counsellors as a source of information for their search.

Research Question

From the literature review, a number of variables may influence students' choice of a university. This study aims to find out what factors influence students' choice of a private university in Malaysia.

Methodology

The study was carried out on a new batch of students enrolling in a Malaysian private university in the second semester of 2016. The sample size consisted of 202 students enrolling in various diploma and degree programs. A self-administered questionnaire was used to collect data from the students. Students were asked to identify and determine the important factors influencing them to choose the university as their choice institution. The questionnaire constitutes 16 factors (program offerings, desired choice, housing, facilities, attraction, teachers profile, reputation, attention received, students' numbers) with response scale ranging from Highly Important 1 to Unimportant 5. The second section of the questionnaire consists of 8 factors (student's choice, parents' choice, self-desire, fees, friends, entry requirements, advertisement, social media) with responses ranging from Strongly Agree 1 to Strongly Disagree 5 (Appendix 1).

Data Analysis

Data analyses involved several procedures conducted using SPSS 17. Data was analysed using factor analysis to determine the underlying components of twenty four items that represented possible preferences for choosing the university. Through factor analysis, a large set of items were scaled down to smaller, more manageable number of items. The reliability test was examined through Cronbach's Alpha Coefficient. The purpose of the reliability test is to measure the internal consistency of the set of items.

Results and Discussions

The first section of the questionnaire showed a Cronbach Alpha of 0.995. This indicated a high level of internal consistency for our scale and meant that respondents who chose high scores for one item also chose high scores for others.

The output from the rotated component matrix which related to the first section of the questionnaire showed that SPSS has extracted 3 factors. The first factor could be classified broadly as Programs and Facilities, the second as Students and Faculty and the third as Curricular Activities. The eigenvalues associated with each factor represent the variance explained by that particular component. Factor 1 explained 41.5% of total variances, followed by factor 2 with 8.9% and factor 3 with 6.4%. All the remaining factors are not significant (Table 1).

The second section of the questionnaire also showed a high level of Cronbach Alpha with 0.72, again indicating a high level of consistency. For the second section of the questionnaire, the factors that load highly on . factor 1 seems to relate to Awareness. The four questions that load highly on factor 1 relate to advertisements, social media and friends. The questions that load highly on factor 2 relate to fees and ease of entry. We could label

Table 1:   Total variance explained.

Component	Initial Eigenvalues			Extraction Sums of Squared Loadings		
	Total	% of Variance	Cumulative %	Total	% of Variance	Cumulative %
1	6.648	41.552	41.552	6.648	41.552	41.552
2	1.428	8.924	50.476	1.428	8.924	50.476
3	1.023	6.396	56.872	1.023	6.396	56.872
4	0.936	5.849	62.720			
5	0.832	5.200	67.921			
6	0.754	4.711	72.631			
7	0.709	4.434	77.065			

Extraction method: Principal component analysis.

Table 2:   Total variance explained.

Component	Initial Eigenvalues			Rotation Sums of Squared Loadings		
	Total	% of Variance	Cumulative %	Total	% of Variance	Cumulative %
1	2.783	34.786	34.786	2.110	26.373	26.373
2	1.240	15.497	50.283	1.913	23.910	50.283
3	0.965	12.069	62.352			
4	0.835	10.438	72.790			
5	0.750	9.378	82.168			
6	0.606	7.579	89.747			
7	0.563	7.034	96.781			
8	0.257	3.219	100.000			

Extraction method: Principal component analysis.

Table 3:   KMO and Bartlett's test.

Kaiser-Meyer-Olkin Measure of Sampling Adequacy		0.895
Bartlett's Test of Sphericity	Approx. Chi-Square	1373.265
	df	120
	Sig.	0.000

this factor Affordability and Accessibility. The eigenvalues associated with factor 1 explained 34% of the variances and factor 2 with 15.5% (Table 2).

Facilities and Program Offerings have a strong association with Factor 1 with loadings of 0.71 and 0.64. Students Numbers and Teachers Reputation are substantially loaded on Factor 2. Curricular Activities and Proximity are substantially loaded on Factor 3. In the second section of the questionnaire, Advertisement and Social Media are substantially loaded on Factor 1 while Fees and Ease of Entry are substantially loaded on Factor 2.

The results of the factor analysis measured by Kaiser–Meyer–Olkin (KMO) for section 1 (0.895) and section 2 (0.711) are both acceptable as they are higher than 0.5 (Tables 3 and 4). This indicates that the data were suitable for factor analysis. From the same tables, we see that the Bartlett's

Table 4:   KMO and Bartlett's Test.

Kaiser–Meyer–Olkin Measure of Sampling Adequacy		0.711
Bartlett's Test of Sphericity	Approx. Chi-Square	335.033
	df	28
	Sig.	0.000

test of Sphericity are significant. That is, the associated probabilities are less than 0.05.

The "means" of the all computed variables were below 3 indicating that most respondents agreed with the importance of the variables in the questionnaire. The variables "choice", "facilities", "proximity" and "ethnicity" ranks the lowest in means scores. The findings revealed that students placed great importance on the availability of good facilities. This is an area which the university management should pay particular attention to. The variable "choice" is closely related to "ethnicity" as the majority of the student population are Chinese and are more comfortable with the Chinese-speaking environment of the university. Students were generally not too concerned with the housing facilities as most of them stay within the proximity of the university or possess their own transport.

Most students rate affordable fees as an important factor. The desire to earn a degree ranks next. However, most students felt that there is a lack of brand awareness through social media and newspaper advertisements. These are areas of concerns as the awareness of the university is generally low. Many students did not hear about the university from their friends. This may be a sign that promotion through word of mouth and referral from alumni is at a low level.

Significance of the Study

The findings of this study will enable the university to make better planning of its student recruitment efforts. With the understanding of the various factors influencing students' choice of a university, university administrators could restrategise their marketing and promotional efforts to compete with other universities in the changing education landscape.

Conclusion

Universities need to remodel themselves in the changing marketplace to maintain connectivity with its various stakeholders: students, staff, faculty, and community. The expectation that university education should be aligned with the market needs implies that universities should promote the career opportunities of their program offerings to their students. Students often consider their prospects of securing employment upon graduation as a proxy of the reputation of their universities.

In line with the changing job market, universities have to introduce new programs which are relevant to the industries. These new programs should focus on developing new skill sets or new knowledge of students in preparation for careers in the changing marketplace. This study reveals that that there are twenty four important factors which influence student choice of a private university. These factors include programs offerings and facilities, composition of students and faculty reputation, and promotional activities and affordability. All these factors comprise a university brand promise. Students are now better informed and are aware of the many alternative universities that they can apply to. The university should take a broader view of branding and not just limit itself to the usual activities of student recruitment, faculty engagement and student experience. It should revamp its brand image to meet the needs of the changing marketplace and to improve the engagement level with both student and staff to enhance their experiences.

One key strategy for the university to differentiate itself is to rebrand its professors. Professors play key roles in delivering the university's brand promise. Distinguished professors could easily become their own brands and become ambassadors of the university. Professors can build the brand as an expert in a particular domain and this in turn can transcend the boundaries of their personal branding to institutional-wide branding. The university should explore and adopt the concept of emotional branding in the changing education landscape. Emotional branding provides the means and methodology for connecting the university products to consumers in an emotionally profound way. It focuses on the desire to transcend personal satisfaction and experience emotional fulfilment. If carried out successfully, emotional branding encourages connectivity and intimacy

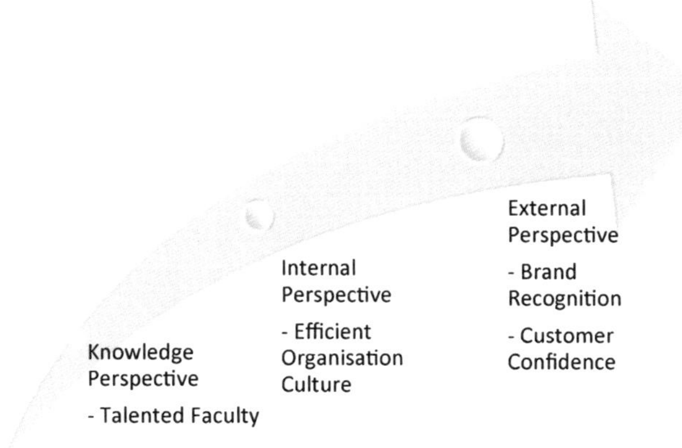

Fig. 2:   Process of rebranding professors.

with the university. This emotional aspect will be the key differentiator between the university and its competitors.

Figure 2 shows the process of rebranding professors. For the rebranding process to be successful, there is a need to have a supportive internal organisational culture to groom and develop talented faculty members. Through this talent identification process, professors who receive support through research funding will be able to promote their personal brand names. With brand recognition through the rebranding of professors, universities can move ahead to reinforce its brand and regain customer confidence.

Limitations of the Study

The sampling process was carried out in one batch of new students in a private university and may not fully reflect the whole student population studying in private universities in Malaysia. Out of the 300 questionnaires handed out, only 202 responded. This may be due to the respondents not having a full understanding of the purpose of the questionnaire or were unwilling to disclose their views and opinions with regard to certain items in the questionnaire.

The gender-blind study also did not investigate if there are any differences between male and female students when choosing universities. These differences may be insignificant as the university provides equal opportunities to all and its marketing and promotional efforts are targeted at all segments rather than to a specific market segment.

References

Abrahamson, T., and Hossler, D. (1990). *Applying Marketing Strategies in Student Recruitment, The Strategic Magement of College Enrollments.* San Francisco, Calif: Jossey-Bass.

Bryman, A., and Bell, E. (2005). *Business Research Methods* (3rd edn.). Oxford University Press, Oxford.

Bourke, A. (2000). A Model of the Determinants of International Trade in Higher Education, *The Service Industries Journal,* **20**(1), pp. 110–38.

Cabrera, A.F., and La Nasa, S.M. (2000). *Understanding the College-Choice Process: New Directions for Institutional Research,* No. 107, San Francisco: Jossey-Bass.

Chapman, R. (1981). A Model of student college choice, *Journal of Higher Education,* **52**, 490–505.

Chapman, R. (1986). Towards a Theory of College Selection: A Model of College Search and Choice Behaviour. *Advances in Consumer Research,* **13**, 246–250.

Chen, L.H. (2008). Internationalization or international marketing? Two frameworks for understanding international student's choice of Canadian universities. *Journal of Marketing for Higher Education,* **18**(1), 1–33.

Choy, S.P., and Ottinger, C. (1998). *Choosing a Postsecondary Institution,* Statistics Analysis Report. Washington, DC: National Center for Educational Statistics.

Cleopatra, V., John, W.L., and Robert, A.P. (2004). University Selection: Information Requirements and Importance. *The International Journal of Educational Management,* **18**(3), 160–171.

Collins, M.L. (1978). Effects of Enthusiasm Training on Preservice Elementary Teachers. *Journal of Teacher Education,* **29**, 53–57. doi: 10.1177/002248717802-900120.

Foskett, N., Maringe, F., and Roberts, D. (2006), Changing fee regimes and their Impact on Student Attitudes to Higher Education, *Higher Education Academy, UK,* **22**(2), 23–31.

Hall, R. (1993). A Framework Linking Intangible Resources: Capabilities to Sustainable Competitive Advantage. *Strategic Management Journal,* **14**, 607–618.

Hearn, J. (1984). The relative roles of academic ascribed and socioeconomic characteristics in college destinations. *Sociology of Education*, **57**, 22–30.

Hossler, D., and Gallagher, K.S. (1987). Studying Student College Choice: A Three-Phase Model and the Implications for Policymakers, *College and University*, **62**(3), 207–222.

Hossler, D., Braxton, J.M., and Coopersmith, G. (1989). Understanding student college choice. In Smart, J.C. (Ed), *Higher Education: Handbook of Theory and Research*. New York: Agathon Press.

Hossler, D., Schmit, J., and Vesper, N. (1999). *Going to College, How Social, Economics, and Educational Factors Influence the Decision Students Make*, The John Hopkins University Press, Baltimore & London.

Houston, M. (1979). Cognitive Structure and Information Search Patterns of Prospective Graduate Business Students, *Advances in Consumer Research*, **7**(10), 552–557.

Jackson, G.A. (1982). Public Efficiency and Public Choice in Higher Education, *Educational Evaluation and Policy Analysis*, **4**(2), 237–247.

John, E.P. (1990). Price Response in Enrolment Decisions: An Analysis of High School and Beyond Sophomore Cohort. *Research in Higher Education*, **31**(2), 161–176.

Joseph, M., and Joseph, B. (1998). Identifying Need of Potential Students in Tertiary Education for Strategy Development. *Quality Assurance in Education*, **6**(2), 90–96.

Kotler, P., and Fox, K.F.A. (1995). *Strateguc Management for Educational Institutions*, Prentice-Hall, Upper Saddle River, NJ.

Krampf, R.F., and Heinlein, A.C. (1981). Developing Marketing Strategies and Tactics in Higher Education Through Target Market Research, *Decision Sciences*, **12**(2), 175–193.

Krone, F., Gilly, M., Zeithaml, V., and Lamb, C. (1983). *Factors Influencing Graduate Business School Decisions*, American Marketing Association Educators Proceedings, Chicago, IL.

Kunter, M., Frenzel, A., Nagy, G., Baumert, J., and Pekrun, R. (2011). Teacher Enthusiasm: Dimensionality and Context Specificity. *Contemporary Educational Psychology*, **36**, 289–301. doi:10.1016/j.cedpsych.2011.07.001.

Leslie, L.L., Johnson, G.P., and Carlson, J. (1997). The Impact of Need-Based Sstudent Air upon the College Attendance Decision, *Journal of Education Finance*, **2**(3), 269–285.

Lin, L. (1997). What are Student Education and Educational Related Needs? *Marketing and Research Today*, **25**(3), 199–212.

Litten, L.H. (1980). Marketing Higher Education. *Journal of Higher Education*, 5(4), 40–59.

Litten, L.H. (1982). Different Strokes in the Application Pool: Some Refinements in a Model of Students Choice. *Journal of Higher Education*, 4, 383–402.

Miles, S.J., and Mangold, G. (2004). A Conceptualization of the Employee Branding Process. *Journal of Relationship Marketing*, 3(2/30), 65–87.

Mourad, M., Ennew, C., and Kortam, W. (2011). Brand Equity in Higher Education. *Marketing Intelligence and Planning Journal*, 29(4), 403–420.

Paramewaran, R., and Glowacka, A.E. (1995). University Image: An Information Processing Perspective. *Journal of Marketing for Higher Education*, 6(2), 41–56.

Price, I., Matzdorf. L., and Agahi, R. (2003). The Impat of Facilities on Student Choice of University, *International Journal of Educational Management*, 21(10), 212–222.

Qureshi, S. (1995). College Accession Research: New Variables in an Old Equation. *Journal of Professional Services Marketing*, 12(2), 163–170.

Sanders, P., and Gosenpud, J. (1986). Perceived Instructor Enthusiasm and Student Achievement. *Developments in Business Simulation and Experential Learning*, 13, 52–55.

Seneca, J., and Taussig, M. (1987). The Effects of Tuition and Financial Aid on the Enrolment Decision at a State University. *Research in Higher Education*, 26, 337–362.

Somers, P., Cofer, J., and Putten, J.V. (1999). *The Influence of Early Aspirations and Attitudes on Postsecondary Attendance*, American Educational Research Association Conference, Montreal, Canada.

Somers, P., Haines, K., and Keene, B. (2006). Toward a theory of choice for community college students. *College Journal of Research and Practice*, 20, 53–67.

Soutar, G., and Turner, J. (2002). Students Preferences for University: A Conjoint Analysis, *The International Journal of Educational Management*, 10(2), 139–146.

Stage, F.K., and Hossler, D. (1989). Differences in Family Influences on College Attendance Plans for Male and Female Ninth Graders, *Research in Higher Education*, 30(3), 301–315.

Stefanie, D., Teresa, L., and Danielle, L. (2006). Higher Education Marketing Concerns: Factors Influence Students' Choice of Colleges, *The Business Review, Cambridge*, 6(2), 101–110.

Tierney, M. (1983). Student College Choice: Toward an Empirical Characterization. *Research in Higher Education*, 8, 271–284.

Tillery, D. (1973). *Distribution and Differentiation of Youth: A Study of Transition From School to College.* Cambridge, MA: Ballinger Publishing Company.

Webb, M. (1993). Variables Influencing Graduate Business Students' College Selections, *College and University*, **68**(1), 38–46.

Yu, S.O. (2016). Reculturing: The key to sustainability of private universities. *International Journal of Education and Research*, 4(3), 353–366.

Appendix 1

WHY I CHOOSE TO STUDY AT THIS UNIVERSITTY

Major (Business, Engineering, Arts, English, etc)   _______________________

Country or State you are from   _______________________

Gender (Circle one)   Male   Female

	Highly Important	Important	Moderately Important	Little Important	Unimportant
SUC offers many Programs					
Found program of my choice					
Availability of Campus Housing					
Good campus facilities					
Campus Attractiveness					
Teacher Profile from website					
Faculty Reputation					
University Reputation					
Personal Attention received from counselors					
Cost of Tuition					
Scholarships availability					

	Highly Important	Important	Moderately Important	Little Important	Unimportant
Ethnic Composition (Chinese, Malay, Indian, etc)					
Location of university					
Near to my home					
Extra Curricular Activities					
Getting part time job on campus					
Possibility to study abroad on exchange program					

	Strongly Agree	Agree	Undecided	Disagree	Strongly Disagree
This university is my choice					
This university is my parents' choice					
My desire to have a college degree					
The tuition fee is cheaper than other universities					
I'm influenced by my friends to join university					
Easy to enter this university					
I learnt about university from advert in newspaper					
I learnt about university from social media					

学而不思则罔, 思而不学则殆

He who learns but does not think, is lost. He who thinks but does not learn is in great danger.

Confucius

Chapter 7

Reframing Absentee Rate

This chapter examines the impact of attendance on student achievement. An analysis of students taking a Statistics course in the third semester of 2015 was carried out to investigate the relationship between class attendance and their final exam grades. Students' achievements were affected by absenteeism from class. The study showed that students who missed classes regularly performed poorly in their final exam. There is a strong correlation between absenteeism rate and failure rate. Students who recorded more than 20% absentee rate in class failed their final exam. This chapter also suggests that we look at *Reframing* as a technique to reduce the non-attendance and to improve students' achievements.

Introduction

The delivery of material in a didactic lecture format is prevalent in almost all university courses. This approach may not be effective for some students as they have different learning styles. The concept of Cognitive Reframing involves changing the person's mental perspective which leads to more positive change. Lecturers and counsellors should help students with poor attendance to identify and restructure their negative and irrational thoughts by replacing them with more realistic and factual information in order to interact well with their learning environment.

One way to reduce the absenteeism rate and to improve student learning is implementing a progressive assessment strategy which consists of a series of assignments, quizzes, tests and presentations, followed by a final exam which carries a lower weightage of the total scores. This strategy will enhance perceived course quality and promotes consistent study habits in students.

University leaders need to relook at strategies to increase student engagement. There has to be a good instructional match between academic tasks and student abilities. The use of media and technology should be encouraged as some students learn better using technology compared with a traditional classroom lecture. Lecturers need to be trained in teaching pedagogies so that they are able to engage students better and to help them see the connections between university life and real-world events. By incorporating the skills for learning, understanding and reasoning, lecturers can improve the cognitive abilities of their students.

Many research studies have shown the close correlation between class attendance and student characteristics. These characteristics include personal discipline, academic motivation, self-evaluation and cognitive ability. Class attendance is a manifestation of student motivation and abilities. Our proposed framework on improvement in student achievement showed that student performance in terms of grade outcome is influenced by internal factors (personal characteristics and motivation), external factors (reframing efforts of lecturers and counsellors) and class attendance. (Fig. 1).

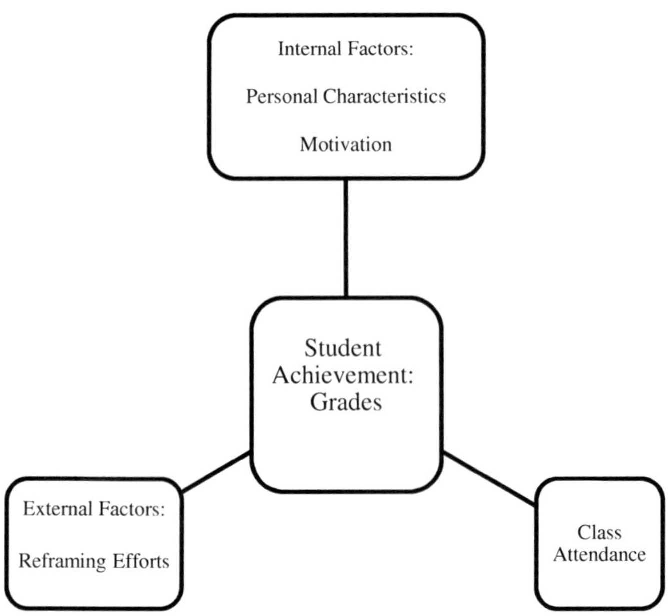

Fig. 1:   Proposed framework for improvement in student achievement.

Literature Review

Cognitive counselling regards thinking errors as the cause for emotional upsets and inappropriate behaviours. Cognitive reframing is a way that we can change our perceptions of stressors and to reduce significant amounts of stress to create a more positive life. It involves changing one's emotion and replacing it with a better one (Jackman and Strobel, 2003).

Kearney and Bates (2001) define school refusal behaviour as the refusal to attend school for an entire day by a child. King and Bernstein (2001) define school refusal as difficulty attending school associated with emotional distress, specifically anxiety and depression. Lauchlan (2003) noted that the problem of school non-attendance is heterogeneous and we should not make unnecessary distinctions when addressing the problem.

The problem of school absenteeism has many negative implications for students who do not attend school regularly. These include poor performance in school, expulsions and dropouts (Petrides *et al.*, 2005). Factors which have identified as causal or correlated to non-attendance include school culture, school environment, poor relationship with teachers and other students, and dissatisfaction with school (Corville-Smith *et al.*, 1998). Higher average school attendance has been associated with higher performance (Roby, 2004). Jones (1984) concluded a negative correlation between absences and grades whereby absenteeism rate correlated with low grades.

Instructors' efficacy plays a large role in course attendance (Romer, 1993). Hansen (1990) found that class attendance was higher when instructors offered a grade point bonus compared to those who did not offer such an incentive. They pointed to the effective use of incentives as a motivator for students to attend classes. Attendance feedback is one technique that could be used to improve student attendance (Gaudine and Saks, 2001). They noted that students attendance improve after receipt of a feedback letter comparing the students absence rate with other students in class.

Davadoss and Foltz (1996) concluded that motivation has a strong impact on attendance rate. However, it has been difficult to determine if attendance rates should be treated as endogenous indicators of inherent motivation or they should be regarded as exogenous indicators. Grump (2004) reported that the highest motivator for attendance was interesting instructor and lecture materials. This conclusion was also supported by

Fjortoft (2005) who noted that teaching effectiveness has an effect on class attendance.

Research Questions

(1) Is there a statistically significant difference in student attendance and student achievement?
(2) Is there a statistically significant difference in student achievement between students with low absenteeism rate and students with high absenteeism rate?

Methodology

The study was carried out on a class of students enrolled in Statistics in the first semester of 2016 at a private university in Malaysia. The sample size consisted of 88 students enrolled at the diploma level. To analyse the relationship between student achievement and attendance, the ANOVA statistics was utilised.

An analysis was carried out to examine how absentee rate (independent variables) may affect exam grades (the dependent variable). We have 4 categories of ordinal variables, namely "No absentee rate" (denoted by 0), "Low absentee rate" (denoted by 1), "Intermediate absentee rate" (denoted by 2), and "High absentee rate" (denoted by 3). Low absentee rate is defined as those absent for 3 hours or less, intermediate absentee rate as those absent between 4 to 6 hours, and high absentee rate as those absent for more than 6 hours.

A significance test was performed to decide if there is any or no evidence to suggest that liner correlation is found in the population. We test the null hypothesis, H_0, that there is no monotonic correlation in the population against the alternative hypothesis, H_1, that there is monotonic correlation.

Let ρs be Spearman's population correlation coefficient, and we can express the test as:

$$H_0: \rho s = 0 \text{ (no monotonic correlation present)}$$
$$H: \rho s \neq 0 \text{ (monotonic correlation present)}$$

Data Analysis and Results

There was a mean difference in the grades between the different groups. Students who attended all classes had a mean grade of 59.04. Students with low absentee rate had a mean grade of 56.7, followed by medium absentee rate with a mean grade of 52.06 and a high absentee rate with a mean grade of 39.4. The results showed that students who had high absentee rate failed their final exam as the passing score was set at 50 points (Table 1).

The output of the ANOVA analysis showed that we have a statistically significant difference between our group means. The significance level of 0.002 is below 0.05, and therefore, there was a statistically significant difference in the mean score between the groups of students with different attendance levels (Table 2).

The Multiple Comparisons table showed which groups differed from each other. There was a significant difference in the exam grades between students who attended all classes and the students with high absentee rate ($p = 0.001$). There was also significant difference in the students with low absentee rate and those with high absentee rate ($p = 0.011$). However, there were no significant differences between the groups with low absentee rate

Table 1:   Grades.

Attendance	Mean	N	Std. Deviation	Minimum	Maximum
0.00	59.0429	35	13.78958	25.00	81.50
1.00	56.7083	24	19.56201	15.50	92.00
2.00	51.9412	17	10.39363	32.00	72.50
3.00	38.5000	12	18.61817	0.00	56.50
Total	54.2330	88	16.89197	0.00	92.00

Table 2:   *ANOVA* grades.

	Sum of Squares	df	Mean Square	F	Sig.
Between Groups	4016.389	3	1338.796	5.405	0.002
Within Groups	20808.085	84	247.715		
Total	24824.474	87			

Table 3:   Multiple Comparisons.
Dependent variable: Grades
Test: Tukey HSD.

(I) Attendance	(J) Attendance	Mean Difference (I–J)	Std. Error	Sig.	95% Confidence Interval	
					Lower Bound	Upper Bound
0.00	1.00	2.33452	4.17122	0.944	−8.5991	13.2682
	2.00	7.10168	4.65286	0.427	−5.0944	19.2978
	3.00	20.54286*	5.26503	0.001	6.7421	34.3436
1.00	0.00	−2.33452	4.17122	0.944	−13.2682	8.5991
	2.00	4.76716	4.98928	0.775	−8.3108	17.8451
	3.00	18.20833*	5.56457	0.008	3.6224	32.7943
2.00	0.00	−7.10168	4.65286	0.427	−19.2978	5.0944
	1.00	−4.76716	4.98928	0.775	−17.8451	8.3108
	3.00	13.44118	5.93417	0.115	−2.1136	28.9959
3.00	0.00	−20.54286*	5.26503	0.001	−34.3436	−6.7421
	1.00	−18.20833*	5.56457	0.008	−32.7943	−3.6224
	2.00	−13.44118	5.93417	0.115	−28.9959	2.1136

*The mean difference is significant at the 0.05 level.

and the group with intermediate absentee rate ($p = 0.799$). There was also no significant difference between the groups with medium absentee rate and the group with high absentee rate ($p = 0.146$) (Table 3).

The Spearman's correlation was used to measure the ordinal scale of attendance. The results presented a Spearman's correlation coefficient of negative 0.375 indicating a fairly weak negative correlation between attendance and grades. The p-value for this test was reported as 0.000, indicating that we have strong evidence to reject the null hypothesis, H_0, in favour of the alternative hypothesis, H_1, i.e. attendance and grades are monotonically correlated (Table 4).

Discussions

The first research question examined the significance of the relationship between student attendance and student achievement. The results revealed

Table 4:   Correlations.

			Grades	Attendance
Spearman's rho	Grades	Correlation coefficient	1.000	−0.375**
		Sig. (2-tailed)		0.000
		N	88	88
	Attendance	Correlation coefficient	−0.375**	1.000
		Sig. (2-tailed)	0.000	
		N	88	88

**Correlation is significant at the 0.01 level (2-tailed).

a fairly weak negative correlation between attendance and exam grades. This suggests that attendance alone does not determine good grades, and other factors such as motivation and self-discipline may play a role. Simply focussing on attendance does not provide the solution to poor academic performance.

The second research question examined the significance of the relationship between students with low absentee rate and those with high absentee rate. The result showed that students who have low absentee rate performed better than students with high absentee rate. While attendance is compulsory, having a graded attendance policy may serve as a motivator for improving class attendance. This approach, together with other continuous assessment methods, may facilitate classroom learning and reduce absenteeism.

Class attendance alone does not guarantee good grades. Both students and lecturers have to be engaged to ensure effective student learning takes place. Students have to take responsibility for their own learning while lecturers are obligated to provide informative materials to keep the students engaged. Lecturers must make students cognisant of the importance of regular attendance. As such, pedagogical approached to education should shift from teacher-centred approach to student-centred approach where active engagement between teacher and student takes place.

Conclusion

This research study suggests that there is a correlation between attendance rate and exam scores, although the correlation is relatively weak. University lecturers and counsellors need to work closely with disengaged students to improve their attendance. This includes talking to students and their families about the students' problems, reframing non-attendance, and re-engaging them to address the absenteeism issue. Giving students feedback in the form of letters informing them of their poor attendance could be a technique to reduce absenteeism. This feedback letter also serves as a form of warning letter informing students that they would be barred from taking exams if their attendance falls below a certain level.

The development of pro-social attitudes and behaviours as well as improving self-discipline will lead the way to improved academic performance of students. However, high-risk students who have no interest in learning will not maintain good attendance despite the efforts of lecturers. More research needs to be done to understand the forces influencing good attendance. With the information, universities can continue to implement policies and practices needed to reduce absenteeism and improve student achievement.

Limitations of the Study

This study has several limitations. The sampling process was carried out in one class of students taking Statistics and more research needs to be conducted to see if the findings are applicable to students enrolled in other programs. It also did not differentiate students who may require some form of incentive to motivate them to attend class from those who are intrinsically motivated to attend class regularly. Further research on the contribution of student attitude and self-discipline will provide additional insights on improving student achievement.

References

Corville-Smith, J., Ryan, B.A., Adams, G.R., and Dalicandro, T. (1998). Distinguishing absentee students from regular attenders: The combined influence of personal, family and school factors. *Journal of Youth and Adolescence*, **27**, 629–640.

Devadoss, S., and Foltz, J. (1996). Evaluation of Factors Influencing Student Class Attendance and Performance. *American Journal of Agricultural Economics*, **78**, 499–507.

Fjortoft, N. (2005). Students' Motivations for Class Attendance. *American Journal of Pharmaceutical Education*, **69**(1), 107–112.

Gaudine, A., and Saks, A. (2001). Effects of an absenteeism feedback intervention on employee absenteeism. *Journal of Organizational Behaviour*, **22**(1), 15–29.

Gump, S.E. (2004). Keep students coming by keeping them interested: Motivators for class attendance. Journal article by Steven E. Gump; *College Student Journal*, **38**(1), 157–160.

Hansen, T.L. (1990). A positive reinforcement program for controlling student absenteeism. *College Student Journal*, **24**, 307–312.

Jackman, J., and Strobel, M. (2003). Fear of feedback. *Harvard Business Review*, **81**, 101–107.

Jones, C.H. (1984). Interaction of absences and grades in a college course. *The Journal of Psychology*, **116**, 133–136.

Kearney, C.A., and Bates, M. (2005). Addressing school refusal behavior: Suggestions for frontline professionals. *Children & Schools*, **27**(4), 208–216.

King, N.J., & Bernstein, G.A. (2001). School refusal in children and adolescents: A review of the past 10 years. *Journal of the American Academy of Child and Adolescent Psychiatry*, **40**(2), 197–205.

Lauchlan, F. (2003). Responding to chronic non-attendance: A review of intervention approaches. *Educational Psychology in Practice*, **19**(2), 133–146.

Petrides, K.V., Chamorro-Premuzic, T., Frederickson, N., and Furnham, A. (2005). Explaining individual differences in scholastic behavior and achievement. *British Journal of Educational Psychology*, **75**, 239–255.

Roby, D.E. (2004). Research on School Attendance and Student Achievement: A Study of Ohio Schools, *Educational Research Quarterly*, **28**, 3–16.

Romer, D. (1993). Do Students Go to Class? Should They? *Journal of Economic Perspectives*, **7**, 167–174.

將欲歙之, 必固張之; 將欲弱之; 必固強之; 將欲廢之,
必固興之; 將欲奪之, 必固與之。 是謂微明。 柔弱勝剛強。
魚不可脫於淵, 國之利器不可以示人。

When one is about to take an inspiration, he is sure to make a (previous) expiration; when he is going to weaken another, he will first strengthen him; when he is going to overthrow another, he will first have raised him up; when he is going to despoil another, he will first have made gifts to him: — this is called 'Hiding the light (of his procedure).'

The soft overcomes the hard; and the weak the strong.

Fishes should not be taken from the deep; instruments for the profit of a state should not be shown to the people.

Dao De Jing

Chapter 8

Reinventing Principal Leadership

This research study was originally conducted in 2009 and some of the literature reviews have since been updated. The author has also injected new discussions and viewpoints to make this chapter more relevant. It examined leadership qualities among private school principals in Singapore. Findings from the study indicate that effective principals are able to establish trust, create structures that promote principal–teacher communication and maintain a high level of moral values. Specifically, it presents the findings from the case of ten private schools in Singapore. The author presents an overview of the study and a discussion of emergent themes and questions related to the roles of the principals and the relations between school and the community. The results from our study indicate that financial goals rank above all other goals set by the private school principals. The emphasis on maximising financial gain is a cause of concern as many school principals have lost their intellectual integrity as well as their academic values in their pursuit of financial gain.

Introduction

This chapter aims to examine the leadership qualities among private school principals in Singapore. It looks at the growth of the Private School industry in Singapore. Data were obtained from field studies as well as published reports of the Government ministries. Specifically, it presents the findings from the case of ten private schools in Singapore. Included is an overview of the study and a discussion of emergent themes and questions related to the roles of the principals and the relations between school and the community. The results corroborate our hypothesis that the private school industry has emerged not only as a complementary sector to the traditional school sector, but also as a profit-making industry. The "profit-making" objectives are causes of concern as many school principals have lost their intellectual integrity as well as their academic values in their pursuit of financial gain.

Effective educational leadership is a concern as private school principals have placed finacial performance as their main goal. The traditional notion of an effective principal displaying visionary leadership, instructional leadership, organisational leaders and collaborative leadership qualities may be lacking in most principals (Fig. 1).

To raise the standards of the private education industry in Singapore, the author propose that school principals and administrators meet certain minimal professional standards before their their applications for renewal as principal or administrator are approved by the regulatory authorities. In other words, the appointment as principal or administrator be limited to a certain number of years, subject to renewal with the approval of the regulatory bodies.

In the first section of this chapter, the researcher summarises the objectives of the study and the research questions. A background of the

Fig. 1:   Effective principal leadership.

private school industry is included. Next, a review of the literature on principal leadership related to professional development and school improvement is discussed. The following section analyses the findings of the study and considers the implications of the analysis for principal leadership and areas for future research.

Objectives of the study

This chapter examines the trends of growth of the private school industry in Singapore and aims to throw some light on the leadership of private school principals. It also looks at factors that have remained the driving force in the development of the private school industry. The main objectives of this study are:

(1) to study the structure and trends in the growth of the private schools in Singapore
(2) to ascertain the leadership qualities of private schools principals, and
(3) to understand the expectations of educational leadership in the private school environment
(4) to determine what factors contributed to the effectiveness of the schools
(5) what quality the principal possesses to lead the school effectively.

Research Questions

(1) What is the state of leadership among private school principals?
(2) What is the principals' perception of their leadership roles?
(3) What are the constraints and difficulties that the principal face when he takes up these leadership roles?

Contributions of the Study

Though this study was conducted in Singapore, its relevance and significance is far from being merely regional. The implications are likely to go beyond geographical, cultural, and social boundaries.

There are a number of potential contributions that this study makes, both theoretical and practical. In theory related issues, the key areas where this study makes a contribution:

(1) Principal Leadership: There are certain attributes that are considered important — personal and professional. The importance of this study is related to professional development of principals of private schools. If principals are able to identify the vital links connecting student learning, staff motivation with principal leadership, they will be better prepared to be leaders. In school improvement and development process, the leadership roles of principals are highly important. Without the changes of the their perceptions of their leadership roles, change will be minimal and difficult. Principals' understanding and perceptions of their own roles in facing new demands in school restructuring are essential for these will affect the outcomes of reforms as their interpretations may shape their role-taking behavior.

(2) Policy-Makers: This study is also helpful in providing policy-makers with certain suggestions to improve the private education sector. The introduction of a certification scheme for private school principals could be considered. Among the criteria to be considered are the qualifications and experience of the principals. Thus, the principal has to become not only a Chief Administrator but also a professional leader. In addition to focusing on profit-generation motives, the principal must create a school culture which promotes teaching and learning. The research findings show that most principals place profit-making as their top priority, above everything else. Policy-makers, however, should be careful not to introduce over-restrictive regulations which may suppress the operations of the private schools. Private schools should be seen as a viable alternative for students who may not be able or do not wish to enrol in the public schools for some reasons.

Background

Enrolment at Singapore's private schools has grown rapidly to 409,479 in 2006. Of this number, 151,430 or 37% are full-time students. There were a total of 1,203 private educational institutions in Singapore of which 642 are commercial schools. The private sector plays a complementary role of running continuing/supplementary education classes in commercial and business studies, computing, language and fine arts courses. Private schools offer courses at the certificate, diploma, bachelor and postgraduate levels. Through collaborations with international universities, private schools offer students the opportunity to attain international certification. In Singapore, only the government universities have the license to issue degrees. Unlike countries such as Australia or Canada, Singapore's private schools do not receive any government funding.

Because there is no government funding, private schools in Singapore do not have to conform to values such as equality of opportunity, the right of all children to a high-quality education, rejection of discrimination and respect for ethnic differences. However, there is a general consensus among owners of private schools that they have a moral obligation to contribute to the development of students as well as to respect for tolerance of difference especially in a multi-cultural, multi-religious nation such as Singapore.

There are mixed feelings as to whether private schools are just enterprises with profit-making as their main motives. Like any private enterprise, private schools strive hard to attract customers and offer them the best possible value.

School choice is transforming the face of education in Singapore with no sign of dissipation. Recent trends indicate that private schools will continue to be an important alternative to traditional schools. The current quantitative query utilised structured interviews with school principals and administrators to find out:

(1) Why students choose private schools?
(2) How private schools compete in the education reform environment?
(3) What contributions that private schools made in Singapore?

The roles of private schools in Singapore

It is widely acknowledged that education is an important source of economic and social development in Singapore. Private schools in Singapore face many disadvantages: lack of funding, low image among local students, and profoundly strict regulatory environment. Yet, despite these obstacles, private schools have managed to survive and thrive, finding a niche for themselves and contributing to the development of Singapore as a global schoolhouse.

The main challenge facing private schools is the bias against private schools. Parents are more likely to send their children to public schools as they have more confidence in the teachers and curriculum of the public schools. As private schools do not receive funding from the government, the question arises as to what extent the government should oversee and regulate the administration of private schools.

Within the education sector, there is some disagreement about the use of the term "private" to describe government-funded institutions. Are institutions such as the Singapore Management University, the Nanyang Academy of Fine Arts or the LaSalle College of the Arts truly private? The degree of public funding should be a important criterion to distinguish between government-funded private institutions and truly private schools which receive no governmental funding at all. Both LaSalle College of the Arts and the Nanyang Academy of Fine Arts received financial support from the Singapore Ministry of Education in the form of polytechnic-level funding for the respective Diploma programme. They are also exempted from the CaseTrust for Education scheme, which the "real" private institutions have to comply with.

In this chapter, we will limit the definition of private schools as those incorporated schools, many of which are companies limited by guarantee with all the assets owned by individuals, companies or religious institutions. The private schools in Singapore cater to both local and international students as well as working adults.

The main advantage of a private school in Singapore is that most private schools feature smaller classroom sizes that allow students to receive much more attention from teachers. Because there is more personal attention given to students, the dropout rates are generally lower.

The diversity landscape in a private school environment provides an invaluable experience to students. Students normally come from different countries bringing along with them the diverse cultures of their respective countries. Students are, therefore, exposed to people from different socio-economic classes, which can broaden their educational experience.

Other possible advantages of private schools include:

(1) Innovation and flexibility — As private schools do not receive state funding, they have more flexibility to develop programs and practices best suited for their students.
(2) Private schools view students and parents as clients. Therefore, they must be more proactive to meet their needs and concerns.
(3) Private schools offer the opportunity for integration of age groupings. Learning is not age-specific and younger students have the opportunity to tap on the experiences of the older students.
(4) Private schools see education as a lifelong process. Because they have a more relaxed guideline on the age of the students, working adults find private schools more accomodating to their learning needs.

Crucial change factors that will guide effective private schools practices:

(1) The principle of self-determination and relative autonomy. School principals need to have increased control over their school strategies and financial health.
(2) The principle of incorporating practical applications with theory.
(3) The principle of promoting schooling as a priority. The issue here is that improvement in socio-economic being is promoted by improvement in education.
(4) The principle of certification and professional development. Private school principals are currently not certified by any regulatory authorities and there is no monitoring of their professional development.

In Singapore, there are no private post-secondary institutions, as the government do not allow private institutions to issue their own degrees. Therefore, the growth of private, for-profit post-secondary institutions is largely absent. This places Singapore at a disadvantage the position behind countries such as United States, Australia, or the United Kingdom where we see private universities have firmly established themselves as being on the move globally. For example, the University of Phoenix has expanded its operations into Brazil, India, the Netherlands, and Mexico.

Literature Review

Leadership is defined as the ability to get all members of the organisation to perform tasks required to achieve the organisation's goals and objectives (Bennis and Nanus, 1985). Good leadership is essential if private schools are to improve. Exemplary leadership creates a sense of excitement about teaching and learning within the school and community by focusing on dreams and expectations of students, parents and the community.

Cuban (1998) refers to leadership as an influence process. Leadership, then refers to how people bend the motivations and actions of others to achieve certain goals. It shows that the process of influence is purposeful in that it is intended to lead to specific outcomes.

Stoll and Fink (1996) use the concept of "invitational" leadership to explain how leaders operate in schools. "Leadership is about communicating invitational messages to individuals and groups with whom leaders interact in order to build and act on a shared and evolving vision of enhanced educational experiences for pupils".

Day, Harris and Hadfield (2001) studied 12 schools in England and Wales which focused on heads who were deemed effective by the Office for Standards in Education (OFSTED). They conclude that good leaders are informed by and communicate clear sets of personal and educational values which represent their moral purposes for the school. The leaders possess the following qualities: respect for others, fairness and equality, caring for the well being and whole development of students and staff, integrity and honesty.

Principals should be able to work with others to implant the vision into the structures and processes of the school. They should be able to communicate to the staff the vision of what their schools should become (Alexander, Rose and Woodhead, 1992). A study by Bolam *et al.* (1993) for the School Management Task Force illustrates a number of problems about the development and articulation of vision in English and Welsh schools. Their study of 12 "effective schools" shows that most school heads were able to describe "some sort of vision" but "they varied in their capacity to articulate the vision and the visions were more or less sophisticated". The study casts doubt on the ability of school heads to communicate the vision effectively and to ensure that it is shared by staff.

Effective leadership involves the alignment of people within the school. Aligning people means getting people to share the same vision and moving forward in the same direction. Aligning people with the same vision and a set of strategies for school improvements help produce the changes needed to cope with the changing environment (Kotter, 1990). Leadership development occurs when individuals become more skilled in getting people to work together as a team and when they have opportunity to develop high-performing work teams. Teams should be the basic unit of performance regardless of the size of the organisations (Kazenbach and Smith, 1993). School leaders must learn not to lead from the apex of the organisational pyramid but from the nexus of a web of interpersonal relationships, with people rather than through them (Murphy, 1992).

Lubienski (2005) concludes that competition in the educational marketplace results more in innovative marketing than in real innovative improvements in instructional practice. A review of the daily Straits Times showed that educational institutions are among the most aggressive advertisers in Singapore. This has also lead to much criticism of the state universities as to whether they should allocate the huge advertising budgets to subsidise students' fees or to carry out more research and development activities.

Private schools in Singapore are all set up by entrepreneurs. These entrepreneurs have to show strong leadership, managerial skills and are generally motivators. Leadership describes the behavior of the school leader by task orientation, relationship orientation and change orientation. Managerial skills refers to the way the school leader resolves problems and make decisions. Motivational skills can be viewed from three dimensions: achievement motivation, affiliation motivation and power motivation.

Many private school principals believe that the growing knowledge about effective education is not well reflected in government policy. The educational outcomes of many of the reforms over the last five years have been disappointing because the reforms have not taken into account the problems faced by private schools. Some school principals contend that recent government policies have deliberately adopted regressive policies that support increased equality between the larger and the smaller private institutions, and also between the government-funded and private institutions. Many educators see politics as antithetical to education and may wish that political pressures might diminish so that they can get on with their work (Levin and Riffel, 1997). This distrust of politics is also one of the motivators to use markets as vehicles to solve educational problems (Plank and Boyd, 1994). This is exactly the case of Singapore private education sector where many schools are subjected to the various competitive forces in the market.

Strategic leadership is the main role of the principal while pedagogical leadership is the responsibility of the teachers (Crowther *et al.*, 2000, 2002; Smylie-Hart, 1999). Their relationships have been described by Crowther *et al.* (2000) as "parallel leadership". Teacher leaders and administrator leaders work in parallel and develop new roles and relationships within the school. Highly effective principals serve as role models for teachers and they are clearly visible throughout the school demonstrating their leadership and particpation in learning activities (Ndiritu *et al.*, 2015).

The influence of transformational leadership is stressed by Geijsel, Sleegers, Leithwood and Jantzi (2001). Their study demonstrates the direct effects of transformational leadership on teachers' commitment to school reform and indirect effects on teachers efforts through teacher motivation. They conclude that the extra commitment and efforts of teachers result in changes in their interactions with students and this have a positive influence on students' outcomes (Geijsel, Sleegers, Leithwood and Jantzi, 2002). Hariri, Moneypenny and Prideaux (2016) found that transformational leadership and rational decision-making are most likely to increase teacher job satisfaction. On the other hand, avoidant decision-making is most likely to reduce teacher job satisfaction.

Change can take place on two levels: the organisational level and the individual level (Kotter, 1996; Lewin, 1952; Richardson and Placier, 2001). Change at the organisational level addresses issues such as organisational development and organisational climate (Senior, 1997). Change at the individual level addresses issues such as motivation, human behavior and beliefs and the relationship of the impact of these beliefs on the organisation (Richardson and Placier, 2001).

The narrow definition focuses on instructional leadership as a separate entity from administration (Murphy, 1988). In the narrow view, instructional leadership is defined as those actions that are directly related to teaching and learning. The broader view entails all leadership activities that affect student learning. Smith and Andrews (1999) conclude that a principal who displays strong instructional leadership usually has the following characteristics:

(1) Places priority on curriculum and instructional issues.
(2) Is dedicated to the goals of the school.
(3) Is able to rally and mobilise resources to accomplish these goals.
(4) Creates a climate of high expectations in the school, characterised by a tone of respect for teachers, students, parents and community.
(5) Continually monitors student progress towards school achievement and teacher effectiveness in meeting those goals.
(6) Effectively hold consultation sessions with faculty and other groups in school decision processes.

Molinaro and Drake (1998) proposed that principals who wish to share leadership must overcome their mindset of "control over" with "support for" teachers and present them with opportunities to grow and develop. Teachers need to have autonomy over instructional practices and be empowered to solve problems. With autonomy and responsibility, the teachers are also held accountable for their actions.

Principals have to possess charismatic qualities. House (1977) noted that charisma influences an affective dimension — the followers look up to and respect the charismatic leaders. Charismatic leaders tend to be energetic, supportive and optimistic (Conger and Kanungo, 1987; Bass 1985). Followers aspire to be like their charismatic leaders, and as a result, this affective process can result in role modeling the behaviour they observe (House, 1977). An underlying assumption in charismatic leadership theories is that they rely on the expressions and alignment of emotions, values and self-concepts between leaders and followers (Connelly, Gaddis and Helton-Fauth, 2002).

Another important aspect of charismatic leadership theories is the identification process (Conger, 1989; Willner, 1968; House, 1977; Shamir, *et al.*, 1993; Bass, 1988). The identification process involves a deeper psychological bond in which it involves more intimate psychological involvement in which the follower's belief about a leader becomes self-defining (Kark, Shamir and Chen, 2003). Followers can project themselves into their leader's situation and likely to experience similar feelings. At the same time, high-impact instructional leaders seek their colleagues agreement about what constitute above-average impacts on student learning (Hattie, 2015).

School leadership is the foremost concern arising from this study. The importance of this concern is reinforced by the recognition of two findings from studies on school improvement:

(a) the realisation that the school is the unit of change (Lezotte, 2005) and;
(b) the importance of principal leadership in promoting participation in school improvement efforts (Taylor and Tashakkori, 1997; Huffman and Jacobson, 2003). As with most school review processes, the measure of school leadership focused on perceptions that staff, parents and students provided.

Leadership requires the principals to accept and promote teachers competence by providing teachers with opportunities to lead. This shifts the traditional hierarchical model in matters relating to teaching and learning. Principals must balance the hierarchical approach of an adhocracy with the hierarchical approach of a bureaucracy (Beairsto, 1999). Principals take on the role of co-learner and collaborator at certain times and that of supervisor and school authority at other times.

Moral leadership assumes that the critical roles focus of leadership ought to be on the values and ethics of principals themselves. Sergiovanni (1984) says that "excellent schools have central zones composed of values and beliefs that take on sacred or cultural characteristics". The moral dimension of leadership is based on "normative rationality; rationality based on what we believe and what we consider to be good."

Methodology

Research methods can be classified as either quantitative or qualitative. The motivation for qualitative method is opposed to that of quantitative method. Qualitative method is designed to help researchers understand people and the social and cultural contexts which they live. Kaplan and Maxwell (1994) argue that the goal of understanding of a phenomenon from viewpoints of participants and its particular social and institutional context is largely lost when textual data is quantified. Qualitative research involves the use of qualitative data such as interviews, documents and participant observations.

The methodology used in this research inquiry is case study. Using multiple sources of qualitative and quantitative data, the study endeavours to examine leadership improvement among private school principals in Singapore. Data collection primarily involves oral narrative inquiry interviews (Clandinin and Connelly, 1999). Narrative inquiry scholars such as Heilbrun (1988) argued that the narrative is "the linguistic form uniquely suited for displaying human existence as situated action".

A series of telephone and face-to-face interviews were conducted with directors, principals and administrators of 15 private schools. The participants in the study consisted of ten practicing principals, three assistant principals, and five key office personnel. The schools offer language courses (six schools) and management courses (seven schools) and arts courses (two schools). Each interview session lasted approximately 60 minutes. The researcher sought to make sense of the respondents' personal stories pertaining to school development and the ways in which these stories intersect (Glesne and Peshkin, 1992). The researcher also sought to understand the respondents' own frame of reference accepting that there were multiple ways of interpreting experiences (Bogdan and Bilken, 1992).

The interview questions were open-ended and guided by a naturalistic inquiry paradigm (Lincoln and Guba, 1985). The questions were open-ended yet specific in intent, allowing individual responses. These questions were reasonably objective, yet allowed for probing, follow-up, and clarification (McMillan, 2000). The interviews were managed as purposeful conversations where their contents and evolution were not defined *a priori*, so that there was variations among the interviews (Paton, 2002). Respondents were not directed by the interviewer, but probes were used to encourage respondents to expand on their thoughts about the private education environment and their experiences within their past and present administrative roles. The pivotal question asked the respondents to reflect on the following question: "from your experience, can you describe the situation of private school leaderships in Singapore" The purpose of this question was to elicit responses that would lead to either areas of concern and proposed strategies to overcome these concerns. The main categories of concern are:

 (1) Instructional leadership — curriculum development, changing evaluation system, professional development and supervision.
 (2) Administrative tasks — providing direction, consultation and contextualising plans and policies.
 (3) Student Issues — Counselling students, developing programs to improve student social interaction and school bullying.
 (4) Human Resource issues — gender issues, teacher stress and teacher harassment.
 (5) Dealing with external agencies — politics.
 (6) Conflict resolution — reducing conflicts between departments.
 (7) Resource Management — program cuts, changing school demographics and fund raising.
 (8) Working with parents — consulting with parents.
 (9) Marketing — promotional activities by the schools.
(10) Opinions on Quality Education.
(11) Strategies and problems encountered in quality education promotion.

The site visits were designed to provide a qualitative understanding of how the individual director, principal and administrator approach the task of managing the school. Topics that have been discussed include how a school defined its goals; how these goals related to its broader mission; how it designed and implemented its strategies; what techniques it used; how it interacted with its broader communities; how it defined and measured progress towards its goals; and what it viewed as major challenges in the industry.

The methodological approach focuses on three distinct phases of the evaluation:

Phase 1: Collection of primary and secondary data

Data were collected and analysed using a variety of qualitative techniques. Among these techniques were document analysis, interviews and questionnaire survey. The primary data is that directly collected from the respondents via the interview. The secondary data is comprised of the reference documents concerning the research subject.

The researcher visited individual schools, explaining clearly to them the objectives of the research and contents of the questionnaires. Each of the participants was interviewed for a period ranging from 15 minutes to half an hour. The scheduled questions were asked and their answers were recorded in writing.

We use existing data on both the national and local levels in our studies. Secondary data sources include:

(1) Bureau of Statistics
(2) Ministry of Education

Phase 2: Analysis of data collected

The study is based on a relative extensive reliance on existing information and data produced at local levels. Information coming from primary sources has been examined taking into consideration the socio-political context of the interviewed person, prior to drawing any final conclusion. Qualitative data analysis is a search for general statements about relationships among categories of data and builds grounded theory from it (Strauss and Corbin, 1997).

The findings were examined using both within-case analysis and cross-case analysis method. Each interview was transcribed and comments were clustered together within a given theme. The research uses both qualitative methods such as open-ended questions and quantitative methods such as requesting respondents to rank their views about a specific question in the questionnaire. The questionnaire is the most widely used type of measure in education. In questionnaire survey, researchers administer questionnaires to some sample of population to learn about the distribution of characteristics, attitudes, or belief (Marshall and Rossman, 1999). Questions are examined for bias, sequence, clarity and validity.

In order to avoid the case when the respondent will be forced to give an inaccurate response when his or her real attitude towards the statements was a natural or middle choice, five responses ranging from 1 = strongly disagree, 2 = disagree, 3 = neutral, 4 = agree and 5 = strongly agree, were given. The statements were scripted as follows:

(1) Teachers will have opportunities to take initiative and lead where appropriate.

(2) Principals will expect teachers to significantly contribute towards improving student learning.
(3) Principals will nurture teachers' capacities to significantly contribute towards student learning.
(4) There is a shared commitment throughout the staff to the achievement of the school's vision.
(5) In the qualitative section of the survey, participants commented upon their expectation as to what leadership skills principals should possess. They are asked to identify the characteristics that would distinguish them, and the attitudes and skills that they themselves expected would define the effectiveness of principals. Questions asked were as follows:

    (a) Identify attitudes that will distinguish these individuals as leaders.
    (b) List the attitudes and skills that will distinguish you most as an effective principal.

The combination of both research methods may be the most effective way for achieving our research objective due to their complementary strengths. It is acknowledged that both quantitative and qualitative analysis suffer from certain specific shortcomings. A mixed methods design aims to combine the advantages of both methods in one single framework.

Findings and Discussions

The schools in this research were mainly small- to medium-sized, with student population of fewer than 250. They are selected consciously and may not be truly representative of the whole private education sector in Singapore. Bearing these limitations, the study nevertheless provides important information both about the constraints faced by private schools and the strategies they adopt in this competitive environment.

It is necessary to describe the characteristics of the schools and the respondents to facilitate a better understanding of the research findings.

(1) Characteristics of the schools.
(2) Characteristics of the respondents.

The three main findings the research questions include:

(1) The state of leadership among private school principals.
(2) The principals' perception of their leadership roles.
(3) The constraints and difficulties that the principal face when he takes up these leadership roles.

The state of leadership among private school principals

Participants' responses were significantly different across the different levels of private schools. As expected, principals feel that they are the most important individual in the organisation. They see "profit motive" as the key objective. This is largely expected as private schools do not receive any funding from the government. The principals feel that there is little need to consult organisational members and normally come up with the final decision alone. This could be due to the differing interests of the principals and the teachers. Teachers normally would want to make requisitions for various equipment (hardware and software) which could make their work easier while principals may see such requests as making unnecessary investment into equipment.

Responses from the other participants (teachers and administrators) describe their principals as:

(1) "having positive attitude" (65%)
(2) "being compassionate" (58%)
(3) "having the ability to communicate clearly the school's vision and mission" (65%)
(4) "possessing the knowledge of curriculum" (60%)
(5) "possessing ethical values and professional behavior" (75%)
(6) "possessing competency as principals" (60%)
(7) "supportive of teachers' needs" (63%)

The principals' perception of their leadership roles

Principals see themselves as:

(1) formal leaders of the schools
(2) possessing positive disposition and being supportive of teachers' needs

(3) having the power to exercise decisions that affect student learning

(4) introducing reforms when necessary

The constraints and difficulties that principals face

(1) Being active listeners, recognising concerns and creating a climate of honesty may sometimes be difficult as any decisions made will have implications on the profitability of the schools. They believe passion, humour and empathy may dilute their authority in the eyes of the students and teachers.

(2) Empowering others through recognition and acceptance may be difficult for some principals who see themselves as having the power to control the teachers and other employees. To them, sharing power and decision-making reflect their own weaknesses. They see soliciting the input of others as a sign of admitting their own incompetencies.

(3) Managing the day-to-day operations of the school has taken up most of their time and there is very little time left for "strategic planning". They see the daily administration, budgeting and managing conflicts as top priorities. Staff training and strategic planning are secondary concerns.

The findings from this study revealed three important strategies that appear to be critical in successfully positioning private schools in an increasingly competitive environment. These include creating a culture of change, valuing collaboration and sharing leadership.

(a) *Creating a culture of change*:
Like all other organisational change, implementing a successful school improvement process is a challenging and demanding tasks. Internal commitment by the school's stakeholders coupled with a strong leadership is the key for the improvement process. Private school improvement efforts include the introduction of new programs and procedures that will transform the schools. New curriculum materials and new methods of instructions are heralded as examples of school improvement. Focusing on school personnel is

the most effective way to improve schools. The key to school improvement is the willingness and ability of principals to assume the role of staff developers. Principals could promote school development by focusing on the professional development of staff and should take into consideration the following:

  (i) Understand the importance of the school's vision, mission and core values.
 (ii) Identify and promote shared values.
(iii) Monitor the critical elements for school improvement.
 (iv) Ensure team effort of every staff member within the organisation.
  (v) Encourage experimentation in methods of instruction.
 (vi) Provide opportunities for staff development.
(vii) Document results.

(b) *Valuing collaboration*:
School management is a more important factor affecting teacher job satisfaction than the physical facilities of the schools. Teachers placed high emphasis on remuneration incentives rather than the professional development as an element of their job satisfaction because most of them do not view the teaching profession as their lifelong career. However, teacher job satisfaction is closely intertwined with non-remunerative incentives such as school management, principal leadership and professional development.

School policies are largely determined by the principals. In all the schools studied, the principals and supervisors are the same person. The principals are the key decision-makers in the schools. Teachers are usually not involved in decision-making processes.

Many private schools see the concept of marketing as indistinguishable from poaching, selling and even deception. There is a close connection between marketing and potential slander of another school. Principals, directors and employees of one school will often belittle another school so that the other school will be viewed by prospective students as of lower quality.

Private schools, due to their smaller student numbers, have better opportunities to offer holistic learning to their students. Holistic learning is an approach to learning that is all inclusive in terms of subject areas and the allocation of sufficient time for learning. It encompasses not only subjects that are measurable but also a more spiritual and ethical depth of learning. According to Duffy (1994), holistic learning includes a world view and a focus on humaneness of the individual. Collaborative leadership involves the following:

(i) A shared vision and shared goals among principals, administrators, faculty and staff are critical for school success.
(ii) Improving education requires a long-term commitment.
(iii) Striving to make continuous changes to improve education.
(iv) Teachers should play an active role in improving the overall school operation.
(v) Every department should collaborate and work closely together to ensure educational quality and employee satisfaction.
(vi) Improvement of quality by using better processes and customer input, rather than imploring teachers to work harder.

Teacher job satisfaction is positively related to participative decision-making and to transformational leadership (Maeroff, 1988). Overall, teachers report greater satisfaction in their work when they perceive their principal as someone who shares information with others and keeps open the channels of communication with teachers.

(c) *Sharing leadership:*
Principals sharing leadership skills with their teachers will enhance overall efficiency of the schools. Many of the performance benefits of sharing leadership are motivational in nature. Leaders help the team to approach the task more effectively by ensuring that there is a high level of commitment among teachers to school objectives. Successful leaders have a strong positive influence on teachers' levels of identification, which in turn fosters teachers' willingness to exert extra efforts to accomplish school goals (Eisenhardt and Tabrizi, 1995).

A number of owners and principals of private schools have no recognised university qualifications and they receive little training as school administrators or as teachers. They are business entrepreneurs who run the schools according to their previous experience. Neale

(1981) has proposed in the Partnership Model of School Improvement, that the principal should play a leading role in a partnership group and be a link to district-level resources and authority. The principal is one of the key elements in identifying local school improvement goals and to plan strategies to achieve these goals. As some of the principals in the sample studied are not trained professionally, they may not be able to utilise their resources effectively for improvement of their schools. Moreover, teachers in private schools are usually not encouraged to take up training. The main reason for this is that almost all the private schools engage part-time contract teachers and do not see training as an important element in their overall school policies. The principals strongly believe that teachers will leave after receiving professional training, thus wasting their financial resources.

Recommendations

(1) The quality of education in private schools can be enhanced in four areas: School Administration and Management, Curriculum, Pastoral Care and Home–School Cooperation. Private school principals should be encouraged to take up training courses to improve their level of competencies to manage the schools properly and have higher sensitivities towards teachers and students. A certification scheme for private school principals should be considered to raise

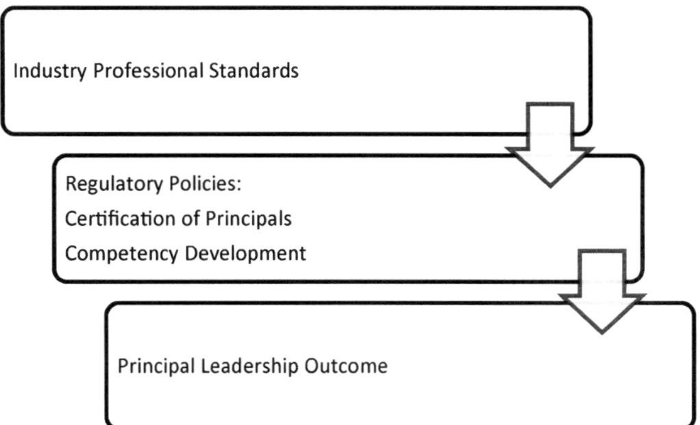

Fig. 2:   Proposed professional standards framework.

the professionalism of principals in Singapore. The school principals need to increase their own knowledge base, in order to respond to new challenges. In addition, a monitoring system of their professional development needs to be in place to ensure continual professional standards are maintained. This could be achieved by requiring principals to meet certain "Competency Development Points" yearly before their licence as principal could be renewed. A proposed Professional Standards Framework could be established to ensure principals and administrators have the competencies to develop the instructional capabilities of teachers and other staff.

(2) Private school principals should move away from school-centred education to learner-centred success and from teaching subjects to teaching learners. The principals should develop a school improvement evaluation plan. Program evaluation plans must be developed and implemented parallel with the action plans and improvement goals. Regular monitoring and assessment need to be introduced to provide a detailed, systematic and ongoing profile of the progress of all students.

(3) End the practice of price competition. Instead of competing on prices, private schools should focus on delivering quality education. Smaller classes, new technology and personalised teaching instructions are a few examples that have long-term positive impacts on student learning. Effective school principals should act ethically to promote student academic success instead of focusing on profits and student enrollment numbers.

(4) Institute a sense of empowerment, growth and self-development for staff. Use evaluation methods for improvement of staff, and not for fault-finding. The principal needs to motivate staff so that they share the vision and mission of the school. They should learn to apply human development theory and motivational theories to the learning process. It is important to draw attention to high expectations and targets as characteristics of effective schools (Mortimore *et al.*, 1988; Sammons, Hillman and Mortimore, 1994). High expectations are assisted by the setting of national or system-level standards that embody challenging goals. These expectations need to be manifested at the level of the school and teachers.

(5) Principals can play a key role in developing teacher leadership. They must see teachers as assets and understand how encouraging teachers

to become leaders will affect their behaviour. They may also have to change their behaviours and be comfortable as facilitators when teachers are leading. However, delegation may be tricky and teachers' willingness to participate sometimes depend on their relationship with the principal. If teachers perceive principals to be open, facilitative and supportive, teacher participation increases (Murphy and Louis, 1994).

(6) Breaking down barriers between classes, levels, departments and administration levels. Teamwork and openness are the key factors of success. Because employee enthusiasm, determination and pride in their jobs will affect the organisation's success, it is important to create an ideal and efficient work medium for staff. Formation of a satisfying institutional climate depends on display of integrity and objective management by the school leader. Principals need to develop the ability to be good listeners. Sustaining reform demands that the principals recognise the legitimacy of everyone's concerns and the value of everyone's resources. The successful principals will take advantage of diversity and view diversity as a resource. They must recognise the strengths of others and utilise them for the good of the private schools. While giving a voice to all people is the foundation of an organisation that is willing to experiment and learn (Heifetz and Laurie, 1997), these voices are often silenced because they create disequilibrium in the organisation. As such, principals must be bold enough to protect these voices so that differing points of view are heard.

(7) More supervision should be given by the Ministry of Education to deter errant players from tarnishing the image of private schools. Regular school visits should be conducted to determine that the schools enroll genuine students and not individuals who hold student visas but do not attend classes. The reputation of the private school industry can be damaged as a result of unethical behaviour. Followers expect their leaders to be trustworthy, honest, open and sincere. The leaders have to display a high level of ethical standards and volunteer for this kind of behaviour (Duncan, 1991). The principals need to possess clear sets of educational and personal values as well as a clear personal vision (Moos, Mahony and Reeves, 1998). Principals need to possess passion, humour and empathy. Good leaders have both wisdom and common sense, and they are viewed as trustworthy and reli-

able. The Ministry of Education should also be more accommodative to private school principals who dare to think "out of the box", taking risks and breaking new grounds. The advantage of private schools as compared to public schools is that business decisions can be made quicker and with less bureaucracy. However, the implementation of such business decisions may often be delayed by the regulatory approvals given by the Ministry.

Private school principals, however, realised that there is no chance whatsoever of politics disappearing from education. The end has been very much in the opposite direction. More regulations are expected to be introduced in the near future to regulate private schools. Educational leadership is evolving to meet with the changes to the educational environment brought on by increasing external pressures from various quarters. The system of evaluation of school principals and teachers need to be in place to ensure that they have the necessary professional development and training to carry out their tasks. Building educational leaders and teacher capabilities is the only way to ensure the integrity of the private education industry.

(8) School principals must create an environment that promotes change. Change is inevitable if schools are going to improve. The principals must exude energy for and commitment to school improvement. They should encourage more communication between them and the various stakeholders — teachers, students, parents, and the community. Teachers have to believe that they can make a difference and have a commitment to do so. Principals have to have the ability to motivate teachers. They have to be able to empower the teachers to a higher level of professional practice and to continuous improvement. Recent research in the field of cognitive science have shown that almost all students can engage in higher-order learning given the right conditions (Odden, 1995). This belief needs to be supported by teachers who have a clear understanding of how students learn. Effective leaders are also able to promote a school environment in which students are encouraged to be an active and responsible member of the school community (Fig. 3).

(9) Principals must be willing to accept the risks and ambiguity that develop as they embrace new visions, based on new knowledge. New ideas may

Fig. 3:   Composition of effective principal leadership.

threaten some staff but they also offer opportunities for those willing to put the visions into practice (Murphy and Louis, 1994). Principals as well as staff must develop a change-enabling culture to adapt to the ever-changing competitive environment. They need to demonstrate that they have the *uplifting leadership* in them (Hargreaves and Boyle, 2015). The term encompasses combining skills that are often set against each other such as pushing and pulling people to change and pursuing long-term sustainability with short-term success.

Limitations

This study had the following limitations:

(1) This study included participants from private schools who are more willing to share their experiences and give their views regarding the private school industry in Singapore. The private schools in this study are considered small with fewer than 200 students each.

(2) The sensitive nature of the information and responses obtained from the respondents may have an effect on participants' responses. Participants may be unwilling to respond to questions relating to their competitive strategies and long-term plans. As private schools are in a competitive relationship among each other, the principals may be unwilling to disclose full information, especially those relating to student numbers, class structure and staff salaries.

(3) The study assumes that teachers' perception of their principals and of their occupation contribute significantly to the explanation of the variance in job satisfaction. However, teachers' perceptions are subjective, and it may be that their perceptions are affected by other variables such as working conditions and salary packages.

(4) The professional values such as integrity and equity are key elements for principal leadership but they do not lend themselves as easily to emprirical research.

Implications for further research

Future research could focus on a larger sample of private schools from a wider variety of backgrounds. It would be interesting to interview parents and students from different schools to gain more insights into their perspectives on their assessments and opinions about these schools. Further studies need to be conducted to look at how leadership training can improve the performance of private school principals. A comprehensive and demanding training of aspiring principals is needed for improvement of leadership preparation in Singapore.

In spite of these limitations, this study provides an important overview of the environment in which private schools operate in Singapore. In general, private school principals have to adopt various strategies which are similar to most private businesses in order to survive in Singapore's competitive environment.

Conclusion

Effective principals are community builders. They are able to nurture the development of open systems in which parents and members of the community are able to voice their opinions. The challenge for most principals is to foster a community of learning among professional staff. They are central agents of change in the system for improving school performance. An effective principal is a necessary precondition for an effective school. The principal's leadership sets the tone of the school, the climate of teaching, the level of professionalism and the morale of the teachers and students. The principals' influence in both the supervisory and instructional domains is strongly related to that of teachers' active participation in decision-making, suggesting the benefits of mutuality in school leadership. As community builders, principals must encourage others to be leaders in their own right.

The most common for all private schools is financial success — a particular profit or return on investment. Other goals may include improving the educational curriculum, providing a conducive environment and developing good teachers and students relationships. To achieve these goals, the principal must set up any number of sub-goals compatible with the primary goals. These tend to be more specific and usually more immediate in nature. For example, to achieve more student enrollment, private schools may offer discounts on school fees or other incentives such as personal computers or PDAs. Private schools principals should focus on improvement strategies which are sustainable in the long-term. Price competition is a short-term approach and can be detrimental over a longer period.

As many of the government regulations, such as the Service Quality Class, seem to impede the development, operations and competitiveness of many private schools, private school principals should be more fully involved in the reforms of the school policies so as to ensure greater adaptability in private school management. They need to have the ability to plan and develop a curriculum that enhances teaching and learning for all students. The ability to use educational research, evaluation and planning process to improve student performance is something that all principals need to focus on.

Principals need to possess a high level of moral leadership. This study suggests that vey often, moral leadership has been compromised for financial gain. Moral leadership acknowledges that values and value judgments are the central elements in the selection, extension and day-to-day realisation of educational purpose (Harlow, 1962). Principals need to possess a portfolio of beliefs and values in issues such as justice, equity, community and schools that function for the main purpose of education. Principals need to engage participants in the organisation and the community in reinterpreting and placing new priorities on guiding values for education. Leadership as moral stewardship means seeing the moral implications of the many daily decisions made by each school administrator (Beck and Murphy, 1994).

Principals need to develop a professional learning community to ensure the sustainability of the school. To be able to achieve this goal, they need to build a school culture and vision that is universally shared by teachers, staff, students and the community. They need to build ethical schools while meeting the moral imperative to provide real learning opportunities to students (Osin and Lesgold, 1996). Principals who become too focused on managing day-to-day activities can unwittingly neglect the important role they can play in helping to create a shared vision for change.

References

Alexander, R., Rose, J., and Woodhead, C. (1992). *Curriculum organization and classroom practice in primary school: A discussion paper.* London: Her Majesty's Stationary Office.

Anderson, L.M., and Turnbull, B.J. (2016). Evaluating and Supporting Principals. *Building a Stronger Principalship,* (Vol. 4).

Bass, B.M. (1985). *Leadership and performance beyond expectations.* New York: Free Press.

Beairsto, B. (1999). Learning to balance bureaucracy and community as an educational administrator. In Beairsto, B., and Ruohotie, P. (Eds.), *The education of educators: enabling professional growth for teachers and administrators.* Tampere, Finland: University of Tampere.

Bennis, W., and Nanus, B. (1985). *Leaders: The strategies for taking charge.* New York: Harper & Row.

Bogdan, R.C., and Bilken, S.K. (1992). *Qualitative research for education* (2nd edn.). Boston: Allyn & Bacon.

Bolam, R., McMahon, A., Pocklington, K., and Weindling, D. (1993). *Effective Management in Schools,* London, HMSO.

Clandinin, D., and Connelly, M. (1999). *Narrative inquiry: Experience and story in qualitative research.* San Francisco: Jossey-Bass.

Conger, J.A., and Kanungo, R.N. (1987). Toward a behavioral theory of charismatic leadership in organizational settings. *Academy of Management Review*, 12(4), 637–647.

Connelly, S., Gaddis, B., and Helton-Fauth, W. (2002). A closer look at the role of emotions in transformational and charismatic leadership. In Avolio, B.J., and Yammarino, F.J. (Eds.), *Transformational and charismatic leadership: The road ahead* (pp. 255–283). Oxford: Elsevier Science Ltd.

Cook, J. (2014). Sustainable School Leadership: The Teachers Perspective. *International Journal of Educational Leadership Preparation*, **9**(1).

Crowther, F., Hann, L., and McMaster, J. (2000). *Leadership for Successful School Innovation: Lessons from the Innovation and Best Practice Project (IBPP)*. A Report from the Innovation and Bets Practice Project (IBPP) to DETYA.

Cuban, L. (1988). *The Managerial Imperative and the Practice of Leadership in Schools*. Albany, NY, State University of New York Press.

Day, C., Harris, A., and Hadfield, M. (2001). Challenging the orthodoxy of effective school leadership, *International Journal of Leadership in Education*, 4(1), 39–56.

Duffy, D. (1994). Holistic Thinking in education in Australia. In Duffy, D., and Duffy, H. (Eds.) *Holistic Education: Some Australian Explorations*. Belconnen, ACT: Australian Curriculum Studies Association (ACSA).

Eisenhardt, K.M., and Tabrizi, B.N. (1995). Accelerating adaptive processes: Product innovation in the global computer industry. *Administrative Science Quarterly*, 40, 84–110.

Geijsel, F., Sleegers, P., Leithwood, K., and Jantzi, D. (2002). Transformational leadership effects on teachers' commitment and effort toward school reform. *Journal of Educational Administration*, **41**(3), 228–256.

Glesne, C., and Peshkin, A. (1992). *Becoming qualitative researcher: An introduction*. New York: Longman.

Hargreaves, A., and Boyle, A. (2015). Uplifting Leadership. *Educational Leadership*, **72**(5), 42–47.

Hariri, H., Monypenny, R., and Prideaux, M. (2016). Teacher-perceived principal leadership styles, decision-making styles and job satisfaction: how congruent are data from indonesia with the Anglophile and Western literature? *School Leadership & Management*, **36**(1), 41–62. doi:10.1080/13632434.2016.1160210.

Harlow, J.G. (1962). Purpose-defining: The central function of the school administrator. In: Culbertson, J.A., and Hencley, S.P. (Eds.), *Preparing administrators: New perspectives*. Columbus, OH: Council of Educational Administration.

Hattie, J. (2015). High-Impact Leadership. *Educational Leadership*, **72**(5), 36–40.

Heifetz, R.A., and Laurie, D.L. (1997). The work of leadership. *Harvard Business Review*, 75(1), 124–134.

Heilbrun, C. (1988). *Writing a woman's life*. New York: Ballantine.

House, R.J. (1977). A 1976 theory of charismatic leadership. In: Hunt, J.G., and Larson, L.L. (Eds.), *Leadership: The cutting edge* (pp. 189–207). Carbondale: Southern Illinois University Press.

Huffman, J.B., and Jacobson, A.L. (2003). Perceptions of professional learning communities. *International Journal of Leadership in Education*, **6**(3), 239–250.

Kaplan, B., and Maxwell, J.A. (1994). Qualitative Research Methods for Evaluation Computer Information Systems. In Anderson, J.G., Aydin, C.E., and Jay, S.J. (Eds.) (1994): *Evaluating Health Care Information System: Methods and Applications*. SAGE. Thousand Oaks, CA, pp. 45–68.

Kark, R., Shamir, B., and Chen, G. (2003). The two faces of transformational leadership: Empowerment and dependency. *Journal of Applied Psychology*, 88, 246–255.

Katzenbach, J.R., and Smith, D.K. (1993). *The wisdom of teams: Creating the high-performance organization*. New York: Harper Collins.

Kotter, J.P. (1990). *A force for change: How leadership differs from management*. New York: Free Press.

Lewin, K. (1952). *Field theory in social science*. London: Tavistock.

Lezotte, L.W. (2005). More effective schools: Professional learning communities in action. In: Dufour, R., Eaker, R., and DuFour, R. (Eds.), *On common ground: The power of professional learning communities* (pp. 177–191). Bloomington, IN: National Educational Service.

Lincoln, Y., and Guba, E. (1985). *Naturalistic inquiry*. Newbury: SAGE.

Lubienski, C. (2005). Public schools in marketized environments: Shifting incentives and unintended consequences of competition-based educational reforms. *American Journal of Education*, **111**, 464–486.

Maeroff, G. (1988). The empowerment of teachers. New York: Teachers College Press.

Marshall, C., and Rossman, G. (2011). *Designing Qualitative Research*, (5th edn.).

McMillan, J.H. (2000). *Essential Assessment Concepts for Teachers & Administrators*. Thousand Oaks, CA: Corwin Press.

Molinaro, V., and Drake, S. (1998). Successful education reform: Lessons for leaders. *International Electronic Journal For Leadership in Learning*, 2(9).

Moos, L., Mahony, P., and Reeves, J. (1998). What teachers, parents, governors and pupils want from their heads, in MacBeath, J. (Ed.), *Effective School Leadership: Responding to Change*, London: Paul Chapman.

Murphy, J. (1992). *The Landscape of Leadership Preparation: Reframing the Education of School Administrators*. Newbury Park: Corwin Press, Inc.

Murphy. J., and Louis, K. (1994). *Reshaping the principalship: Insights from transformational reform efforts.* Thousand Oaks, CA: Corwin Press.

Neale, D., Bailey, W., and Ross, B. (1981). *Strategies for School Improvement.* Allyn and Bacon, Inc., London.

Ndritu, A., Gikonyo, N., and Kimani, G. (2016). Preaching and Drinking Wine: A Necessity for Transformational Leaders in Effective Schools. *International Journal of Education and Research,* **3**(3), 1–10.

Odden, A. (1995). *Educational Leadership for America's schools.* New York: McGraw-Hill Inc.

Osin, L., and Lesgold, A. (1996). A proposal for reengineering of the educational system. *Review of Educational Research,* **66**, 621–656.

Paton, M.Q. (2002), *Qualitative evaluation and research methods* (2nd edn.). Newbury Park: SAGE Publications.

Richardson, V., and Placier, P. (2001). *Teacher change. Handbook of research on teaching* (pp. 905–947). Washington, DC: American Educational Research Association.

Rossmiller, R.A. (1992). The secondary school principal and teachers' quality of work life. *Educational Management and Administration,* **20**(3), 132–146.

Rostker, L.E. (1945). The measurement of teaching ability. *Journal of Experimental Education,* **14**, 5–51.

Sammons, P., Stoll, L., Lewis, D., and Ecob, R. (1988). School Matters: the junior years. London: Paul Chapman.

Sammons, P., Hillman, J., and Mortimore, P. (1994). *Key characteristics of effective schools: A review of school effectiveness research.* London: Office for Standards in Education (OFSTED).

Senior, B. (1997). *Organisational change.* London: Prentice Hall.

Sergiovanni, T. (1984). Leadership and excellence in schooling, *Educational Leadership,* 41(5), 4–13.

Smith, W., and R. Andrews. (1989). *Instructional Leadership — How Principals Make a Diiference,* ASCD, Alexandria, Virginia.

Smylie, M., and Hart, A. (1999). School leadership for teacher learning and change — A human and social capital development perspectives. In *Handbook on Research on Educational Administration,* pp. 421–41. San Francisco, CA: Jossey-Bass.

Stoll, L., and Fink, D. (1996). *Changing our Schools,* Milton Keynes: Open University Press.

Strauss, A., and Corbin, J. (1990). *Basics of qualitative research: Grounded theory procedures and techniques.* Newbury Park, CA: SAGE Publications, Inc.

Taylor, D., and Tashakkori, A. (1997). Toward an understanding of teachers desire for participation in decision-making. *Journal of School Leadership,* 7, 609–628.